Alphonse Daudet

Thirty Years of Paris And of My Literary Life

Alphonse Daudet

Thirty Years of Paris And of My Literary Life

ISBN/EAN: 9783744695008

Printed in Europe, USA, Canada, Australia, Japan

Cover: Foto ©Thomas Meinert / pixelio.de

More available books at **www.hansebooks.com**

Thirty Years
of Paris

GEORGE ROUTLEDGE AND SONS

LONDON, GLASGOW & NEW YORK

ALPHONSE DAUDET.

Thirty Years of Paris

ALPHONSE DAUDET

Thirty Years of Paris

and

Of my Literary Life

ILLUSTRATED

By Bieler, Montégut, Myrbach, Picard and Rossi

Translated by Laura Ensor

LONDON

GEORGE ROUTLEDGE AND SONS

BROADWAY, LUDGATE HILL

GLASGOW AND NEW YORK

—

1888

CONTENTS.

THE ARRIVAL.

WHAT a journey it was! At the mere recollection of it, after thirty years, I can again feel the sensation of cramp, and again my legs seem to be imprisoned in fetters of ice. For two days I was cooped up in a third-class carriage, in light summer clothing, in bitterly cold weather!

I was just sixteen; I came from far away, from the furthest corner of Languedoc, where I had been usher in a school. I was coming to Paris, in order to devote myself to literary

B

work! When I had paid my railway fare, I
was left with the exact sum of forty sous in
my pocket!

But why should I be worried or anxious?
Was I not rich in anticipation? I even
forgot to be hungry, notwithstanding the
tempting array of tarts and sandwiches which
decked the buffets at the railway stations; I
was determined not to change that precious
coin carefully hidden away in the innermost
recesses of my pocket. However, towards
the end of our journey, when our train,
groaning and tossing us from side to side,
was bearing us across the dreary plains of
the flat Champagne country, I very nearly
fainted. My travelling companions, sailors,
who had been whiling away the time with
singing, offered me a flask. What fine
fellows! How harmonious seemed their
rude ditties! and how good their rough brandy
to one who had not tasted food for eight and
forty hours!

It saved and reinvigorated me, and, overcome by fatigue, I leant back and dozed off.
A sleep, however, broken by periodical
awakenings when the train stopped, and

painfully resumed when it had started again. . . . .

At last, a sound of wheels clanking on the turn-tables, a gigantic glass dome overhead blazing with light, doors banging, luggage vans clattering on the pavement, a restless busy crowd, customhouse officers—in fact, Paris.

My brother was waiting for me on the platform, a knowing, sharp, practical fellow, in spite of his youth, and fully alive to the importance of his duties as an elder brother, he had secured a hand-cart and engaged a *commissionaire*.

" He will carry away your luggage."

It was a load that luggage ! A poor little trunk studded with nails, patched all over, and weighing more in itself than all its contents. We started off in the direction of the Quartier Latin, along the deserted quay, through the slumbering streets, walking behind the porter, who was pushing the hand-barrow. It was scarcely daylight, we only met some workmen, their faces blue with cold, or newspaper hawkers, who were cleverly slipping the morning papers beneath

the house doors. The gas lamps were ex-
tinguished, and the streets—the Seine being
at its highest—all appeared to me gloomy
through the grey morning mist. Such was

my entry into Paris. Clinging to my brother,
my heart full of anxiety, I experienced a
feeling of involuntary terror while we continued steadily following the cart.

" If you are not in too great a hurry to see our room, we will breakfast first," said Ernest.

" Oh yes, by all means."

I was literally dying of hunger.

But alas! the coffee tavern, one in the rue de Corneille, was not yet opened; and we had to wait a long time, trying to keep ourselves warm by walking about the neighbourhood, and round the Odéon, which impressed me by its huge roof, its portico, and its temple-like appearance.

At length the shutters were flung back and a sleepy-looking waiter admitted us, noisily dragging his loose slippers across the floor and muttering to himself, very much in the way that stable-men do when awakened from

their sleep to put to the relays. Never shall I forget that breakfast in the dawning light. I have but to close my eyes for the whole scene to reappear before me. The bare white-washed walls, dotted with rows of pegs, the bar covered with piles of napkins rolled in their rings, marble tables without table-cloths, but scrupulously clean, glasses, salt-cellars, and tiny flasks filled with wine, in which there was not a drop of grape juice, but which to me appeared excellent—all these were already in their places.

"Three sous of coffee" the waiter called out on his own responsibility directly he saw us, and as at this early hour there was no one else but himself in the place, he answered "Boum" to himself, and brought us "*three of coffee,*" that is to say, three sous worth of delicious, fragrant coffee, tolerably sweet: which soon vanished, as well as two small loaves that he had brought in a little basket.

We then ordered an omelette, for it was too early to be able to get a cutlet.

"An omelette for two."

"Boum," bellowed the waiter.

"And well done !" cried my brother.

I was overcome with respectful emotion at the coolness and lordly airs of my sybarite of a brother. And at dessert, eyes fixed upon eyes, elbows on the table, what schemes, what confidences, did we not exchange, as we sat with a plateful of raisins and nuts before us! He who has well dined is a better man! Away with melancholy and anxiety; this simple breakfast had intoxicated me as much as champagne.

We sallied forth arm in arm, talking at the top of our voices. By that time it was broad daylight. Paris beamed upon me through her open shop windows; the Odéon itself seemed to nod affably towards me; and the white marble queens in the gardens of the Luxembourg, that I caught sight of through the railings in the midst of the leafless branches, appeared to bow graciously and welcome my arrival. My brother was rich! He filled the post of secretary to an old gentleman who was dictating his memoirs and gave him a salary of seventy-five francs a month. Till I should win my laurels, we had to live on these seventy-five francs a month, and to share the tiny room on the fifth floor, almost a garret, in the

Hôtel du Sénat, rue de Tournon, which however seemed to me a palace. A Parisian attic !
The mere sight of those words " *Hôtel du
Sénat* " staring in big letters on the front of
the house, flattered my conceit, and dazzled
my mind. Opposite the hotel, on the other
side of the street, there
was an old house, dating
from the last century,
with a pediment and
two reclining figures,
which always gave me
the impression that they
were about to fall from
off the wall into the
street below.

" That is where Ricord
lives, said my brother,
the famous Ricord, the
Emperor's physician."

The Hôtel du Sénat ! the Emperor's doctor !
These grand words delighted me and tickled
my vanity. Oh, those first impressions of
Paris.

The large restaurants of the Boulevard St.
Michel, the new buildings on the boulevard

St. Germain and in the rue des Écoles had
not yet driven away the studious youth of the
Quartier Latin, and in spite of its high
sounding name, our hotel in the rue de
Tournon did not pique itself on its senatorial
gravity.

There was quite a colony of students there,

a horde from the south of Gascony, fine
fellows, slightly vain-glorious and self sufficient, but jovial withal, great beer drinkers
and palaverers, who filled the staircase
and passages with the deep tones of their
sonorous bass voices. They spent their time
in empty talk and endless argument. We

B 2

seldom met them, only on Sundays, and then
by chance; **that is** to say, when our purses
allowed us the luxury of a dinner at the *table
d'hôte.*

It was there that I first saw Gambetta.
He **was even** then the man we have all
known and admired. Rejoicing in life; rejoicing in talk; **this loquacious** Roman grafted
**on a Gallic stock, intoxicated himself with the
jingle of** his own phrases, **making the window
panes vibrate with the** noise **of his** thundering
eloquence, most frequently ending in exuber-
ant explosions **of mirth.** Already he reigned
supreme over **the** mass of his comrades. **In**
the **Quartier Latin,** he was **an** important
personality, all **the** more so that he received
three hundred **francs a** month **from** Cahors—
**an enormous sum for a student in' those
remote days.** Later on we became intimate,
but at that time I was only a raw provincial
lad, new to Paris, **and I** was satisfied to sit
at the further end of the table and contem-
plate him from afar with a feeling of admiration unclouded by the faintest shadow of
envy.

Both he and his friends were wholly absorbed in politics, and from the Quartier Latin, they were already laying siege to the Tuileries, while my tastes and ambition were directed towards other conquests. A literary life was the sole object of my dreams. Sustained by the boundless confidence of youth, poor but radiant, I passed the whole year in my attic, versifying.

It is an ordinary and touching story. Paris can reckon hundreds of poor young fellows, possessors of no other fortune than a few rhymes; but I do not imagine that any one ever began his career in destitution more complete than mine.

With the exception of my brother, I knew nobody. Short-sighted, awkward, and timid, whenever I stole forth from my garret, I invariably wandered round the Odéon, strolling beneath its arcades, overcome by fear and joy at the idea that I might meet some literary character—near Mme. Gaut's shop, for instance. Mme. Gaut, already an old woman, but with astounding eyes, brilliant and black, allowed me to glance over the new works exposed for sale, on condition that I did not cut the leaves.

Often I saw her conversing with the great
novelist, Barbey d'Aurevilly, and while she
knitted a stocking, the author of *Une Vieille
Maitresse* stood before her with his hand

on his hips, *à la Mérovingienne,* the end of
his waggoner's cloak, lined with handsome
black velvet, thrown over his shoulder, so
that all might behold the richness of the
apparently unpretending garment.

Some one approaches, 'tis Vallès. The
future Communist passed nearly every day
in front of Madame Gaut's establishment, on

returning from the reading room of " la Mère
Morel," where it was his daily habit to go
betimes in the morning to work and read.
Cynical, caustic and eloquent, always arrayed

in the same old frock coat, he spoke in a
harsh, metallic voice, apparently issuing from
the depths of a rough, bristling beard, which,
reaching **nearly to** the eyebrows, enveloped
his sombre **Auvergnat** physiognomy. This
voice grated on my nerves. He had recently
written *L'Argent,* a pamphlet dedicated to
Mirès, and illustrated in vignette form with a
design representing **a five franc** piece; and
while waiting **to** become **the** associate of
Mirès, he was the inseparable companion of
the old critic, Gustave Planche. **The
Aristarchus of** the *Revue des Deux-Mondes*
was at that time a ponderous old man of
stern **mien,** an inflated Philoctetes, with a
shuffling and limping gait. **One** day I had
the audacity to play the spy upon them from
a window of the café of the Rue Taranne, by
raising myself **up to the** casement and **rubbing the** pane with my fingers; it was the café
next to the house—now demolished—**in**
which Diderot lived for forty years. They
were seated facing each other, Vallès gesticulating vehemently, and Planche rapidly
emptying a small flask of brandy—tossing
down glass after glass.

Neither can I forget Cressot, the easy-tempered, eccentric Cressot, whom Vallès has since rendered immortal in his *Réfractaires!* How often I saw him gliding through the streets of the Quartier Latin, with his sad and suffering face, and his thin, lanky form shrouded in a short cloak.

Cressot was the author of *Antonia*, a poem. No one knew how the poor devil subsisted. One fine day however a friend in the provinces left him a small annuity : that day Cressot dined,—and died of it.

Yet another face of this period is also graven on my memory; that of Jules de la Madelène one of the best *poetæ minores* of our prose literature, the author of works too little known, which excel by the beauty of their truly classical style : the *Âmes en Peine* and *Le Marquis de Saffras.* Of aristocratic manners, and a blonde type of head, recalling by its delicate and somewhat pallid features, Tintoretto's *Christ,* his eyes seemed always full of sadness, and longing for the warm sun of his native country, Provence. The romance of his life was told in whispers : 'twas that of an enthusiast, and a brave scion

of good family. Severely wounded on the
barricades in June, 1848, he had been left for
dead amongst the fallen insurgents. Picked
up by a tradesman, he remained concealed
in the house of his rescuer, whose family
nursed him devotedly till he was restored to
health, when he married the daughter of his
host.

To meet these celebrated men, and perchance exchange a few words with them, was
sufficient to fire me with ambition, and I
boldly exclaimed " I too will be famous ! "

With what impetuous eagerness I rushed
up the five flights of stairs,—especially
when I had managed to buy a candle which
enabled me to work all night, and by the

light of its flickering flame, elaborate verses,
and sketch out dramas, covering innumerable
sheets of paper in endless succession.
Audacity lent me wings; I saw a magnificent
future opening before me, I forgot my pov-

erty; I forgot my privations; as on that well-
remembered Christmas Eve when I, rapidly
penning my rhymes, heard far below me the
noisy festivities of the students, amongst
whom dominated the voice of Gambetta,

thundering through the hall and re-echoing along the passages, causing even my frozen window-panes to vibrate.

But once in the streets, all my former fears returned.

The Odéon in particular filled me with awe. During the whole of that year it seemed to remain as frigid, as imposing and inaccessible as it had first appeared to me on the day of my arrival. Odéon! Mecca that I yearned for, object of my secret aspirations, how often did I repeat my timid and ineffectual attempts to cross the sacred threshold of the small low doorway through which thine artists entered!

How often did I watch Tisserand in all his glory pass through that portal, rounding his shoulders under his cloak in the awkward and careless fashion affected by Frédérick Lemaître! After him, arm in arm with Flaubert, and as like him as a brother, came Louis Bouilhet, the author of *Madame de Montarcy;* followed frequently by Count d'Osmoy, now a deputy. They were at that time writing together, a grand fantastic piece, which however was never produced on the stage. Behind them again, all cast in the same dragoon mould, adorned with fair moustachios, came a group of four or five gigantic Normans. This was the cohort from Rouen, Bouilhet's faithful lieutenants, who applauded to order, the first represent-ations of his plays.

Then Amédée Rolland, Jean Duboys and Bataille followed on, a younger, more enter-prising and daring trio; striving also to enter by that little door, under the ample shelter of Tisserand's cloak.

All three, like Bouilhet, died at the outset of their literary career, and thus it is that the arcades of the Odéon, as I wander through them in the twilight are to me peopled with friendly shades.

However, having completed a small volume of poems, I went the round of the publishers. I called on Michel Lévy, on Hachette. Where did I not venture! I stole in and out of all the large publishing offices, vast as cathedrals, and in which, notwithstanding the carpets, the creaking of my boots made a terrible noise. Clerks with bureaucratic airs stared at me in a chilling and consequential manner.

"Could I see M. Lévy?—about a manuscript."

"I will see, sir. Kindly give me your name."

On hearing the name, the clerk methodically put his lips to one of the speaking tubes
and applied his ear to the other.

"M. Lévy is not in."

M. Lévy never was in, neither was M.

Hachette; no one ever was in, and always
thanks to that odious speaking tube.

The Librairie Nouvelle, in the Boulevard
des Italiens, still remained for me to try.
There I found no speaking tube, no official
staff—nothing of the kind. The publisher
Jacotet, who was then starting his new series
of little volumes at one franc apiece—an

idea of his own—was a short, small man,
reminding one of Balzac, but without Balzac's
noble brow ; constantly in motion, overwhelmed by business and dinner-parties, and

continually planning some vast scheme. His
money burnt in his pockets. In a couple of
years this restless activity brought him to
bankruptcy, and he left France to found the
newspaper *L'Italia,* on the other side of the

Alps.   His establishment was the rendezvous for all the choice intellects of the boulevards, and here might be seen Noriac, who
had just published his 101ᵉ *Régiment;*
Scholl, happy and proud at the success of his
Denise; Adolphe Gaiffe and Aubryet.   All
these frequenters of the boulevards, irre-
proachably " got up," gossiping about women
and money, made me feel shy and awkward
when I caught sight of my own figure, reflected amongst theirs, in the glass of the
shop windows, with my hair as long as a
pifferaro's, and my little Provençal headgear.
As for Jacotet, he was constantly making ap-
pointments to meet me at three o'clock at
the Maison d'Or.

" We will talk over matters," he would say,
"and sign our agreement on the corner of the
table."

What a humbug! I hardly knew where
his Maison d'Or was! Nevertheless my
brother encouraged me a good deal when I
returned home on the verge of despair.

One evening however I was the bearer
of a grand piece of news and a great joy !
The *Spectateur,* a legitimist paper, had agreed

to test my talents as a journalist. It is easy
to fancy with what affection and tender care
I wrote my first article, bestowing a scrupulous attention even on the caligraphic part of
the work! I carried it to the office, it was
read, approved of, and sent to the printers.
I waited breathlessly for the number to
appear. Suddenly Paris was turned upside
down! Some Italians had fired at the
Emperor.

Paris was immediately terrorized, the
papers were prosecuted, and the *Spectateur*
suppressed. Orsini's bomb had blown up
my article!

I did not kill myself, but I thought of
suicide. Heaven, however, kindly took pity
on my woes, and I discovered the publisher
whom I had so long sought for far and near,
at my very door. It was Tardieu, the publisher in the rue de Tournon.

Himself a literary man, his compositions,
Mignon, and *Pour une Épingle,* written in
sentimental sugar and water style, had met
with some success. I made his acquaintance
by accident one evening when he happened
to seat himself in front of his shop, while I

was loitering about near our hotel. He published my *Amoureuses.*

The title was attractive, the volume prettily got up. Both my production and myself were noticed by the papers, and now all my shyness seemed to vanish.

I boldly walked about under the arcades of the Odéon, watching how the sale of my book progressed, and still more audacious, at the end of a few days I even ventured to speak to Jules Vallès. I had appeared in print.

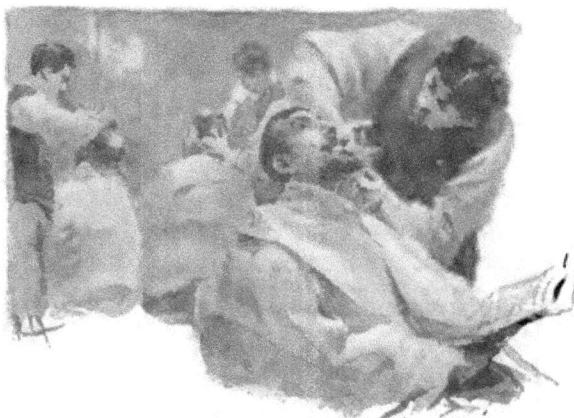

VILLEMESSANT.[1]

I GO sometimes, when my personal requirements and the direction of my walks chance
to coincide, and have my beard trimmed or
my hair cut at Lespès. A very interesting and
truly Parisian nook is this large barber's shop,
occupying the entire angle of the Maison
Frascati, between the rue Vivienne and the
Boulevard Montmartre. As patrons, Lespès

[1] Written in 1879.

had "all Paris", that is to say, that infinitesi-
mal number of Parisians, whose existence
begins and ends with the Gymnase and the
Opera, Notre Dame de Lorette, and the
Bourse, and who fancy that they alone exist!
Then he had the stockbrokers, the actors,
the journalists, without reckoning the innumerable legion of busy, fussy idlers and
frequenters of the Boulevards. Twenty or
thirty barbers are in constant work, curling
and shaving all day.

Superintending everything, keeping a sharp
eye on the razors and pomatum pots, continually moving from room to room, Lespès, the
proprietor, is a small, vivacious man, who, his
fortune made (and he is very wealthy), would
have grown fat, were it not that a certain
disappointed ambition keeps him in a continual state of fever. It was in this house,
really predestined, that, twenty years ago, in
the very *entresol* where Lespès carries on
his business, the *Figaro* had its offices.
Here was the lobby, the subscription room,
the cashier's office, where from behind a wire
grating peered the round eyes and sharp
beak of old Legendre, always irritable,

seldom amiable, like a parrot turned cashier.
Here was the editorial room, with "No
admittance except on business" written on
the ground glass of the door, and inside, a
few chairs ranged round a large table covered
with an immense green cloth. I can still see
it all, and can see myself, timidly sitting in a
corner, hugging under my arm my first article,
rolled and tied up with tender and affectionate care. Villemessant had not yet returned.
They had told me to wait, and I was waiting.
On that occasion there were about half-a-
dozen men seated round the green clothed
table, skimming the papers, or scribbling.
They were laughing and talking, smoking
cigarettes, and matters were being merrily
discussed. Amongst them was a small
man with a red face, and white hair
brushed up on end, making him look like
a cockatoo.

This was M. Paul d'Ivoy, the celebrated
chronicler, who had been enticed away from
the *Courrier de Paris* regardless of cost—
Paul d'Ivoy, whose fabulously large remuner-
ation (it was fabulous at that time, but would
not appear so now) made him the admiration

of all the literary circles.   He wrote with a
smile upon his face, like a man thoroughly
pleased with himself: the slips of paper grew
black under his pen, and I sat by, watching
M. Paul d'Ivoy smiling and writing.

All at once there was a sound of heavy
footsteps, and a thickened, jovial voice:

" Villemessant ! "   Instantly the pens
scratched away, the laughter ceased, and
the cigarettes were hidden, Paul d'Ivoy
alone raised his head and dared to gaze
familiarly upon their imposing deity.

VILLEMESSANT : " That's right, my children,
I see that you are all hard at work."   (*To*

Paul d'Ivoy in a good-natured manner):
" Are you satisfied with your article ? "

PAUL D'IVOY: " I think it will do."

VILLEMESSANT: "Well so much the better,
that is lucky, for it will be your last."

PAUL D'IVOY (*turning pale*) : " My
last ? "

VILLEMESSANT : Certainly ! I am not laugh-

ing—your writings are most tedious—there
is but one opinion on the Boulevards—you
have bored us long enough."

Paul d'Ivoy had risen from his chair:
" But our agreement, sir ?—Our agreement ? "

" That's a good joke ! Just try and bring
an action against me—that would be fun :
I should read aloud your contributions in
open court, and we should soon see if any
agreement could compel me to insert such
rubbish in my paper ! " Villemessant was
quite capable of carrying out his threat, and
Paul d'Ivoy never went to law. All the same,
this way of shaking off his officials with as
little ceremony as an old carpet out of a
window, gave poor innocent me cold shivers !
I began to wish both myself and my hapless
manuscript, so ridiculously rolled up, a hundred
feet under-ground. I never entirely got over
that first impression ; after this I often met
Villemessant, and he was always most kind,
but I invariably felt on seeing him the same
cold shudder of painful terror that Hop o' my
Thumb must have experienced on first
meeting the Giant.

To be quite fair, I am bound to add that

when in after days, this same Paul d'Ivoy,—
so summarily dismissed—died, it was
Villemessant, real ogre and St. Vincent de
Paul in one, who voluntarily provided for the
education of his children.

Was he kind or was he cruel? It is a
puzzling question, and Diderot's comedy
seems to have been written on him. Kind,
he certainly was, and cruel too, according to
his passing fancy; and a painter might, without falsifying a line, or a shade, have drawn
two portraits of him : one kind and benevo-
lent, the other harsh and cruel ; one all black,
the other all bright and rose-coloured, which,
though bearing no resemblance to each other,
would both be an excellent likeness of the
original.

In relating characteristic anecdotes of this
singularly dual nature, the only difficulty
which arises, proceeds from their excessive
variety.

Before the war, I had made the acquaintance of a good honest man, father of a
family, a clerk at the Central Post Office, rue
Jean Jacques Rousseau. When the commune broke out, he remained in Paris.

Possibly there lurked in the secret recesses of
his heart a weakness for the insurrection, of
that I cannot feel sure.   Perhaps he said to
himself that after all, as letters would continue

to arrive in Paris, some one must sort and
distribute them ; that is perfectly probable. It
may have been that, encumbered with a wife
and grown up daughters, a sudden exit was
not within his means.   At that moment Paris

could reckon many a poor devil in a similar position, barricaders through the force of circumstances, insurgents without knowing

wherefore. However that may have been, notwithstanding M. Thiers' orders, my friend remained at this work, behind his grating,

c

methodically sorting his letters amid the noise
of battle, **as if** nothing unusual were hap-
pening; but he absolutely refused to accept
any promotion **or increase of pay** from **the**
Commune. Nevertheless, when the **Commune** was put down, he was dismissed, **and**
—too thankful to escape being tried **by court-**
martial—found himself thrown destitute **on**
the streets, when **on the very** eve **of** obtain- .
ing **a** pension. **Henceforth** an existence **at**
once sad and comical began for him. **He**
had **not dared to** inform his family of his
dismissal; **each** · **morning his** daughters
prepared **a clean starched** shirt for him (a
government official must **be neat** !), carefully
and merrily, as **in** former days, tied the bow
of his cravat, **and** kissed him at the door as
they bid him good-bye at the usual hour,
fancying he was going to his office. His
office ! Ah, now far away was that office ! **so
cool in** the hot summer, so well warmed in **the**
cold winter—that office **where** the time used
to pass so peacefully. **Now he was** obliged
to tramp all over Paris through **rain** and snow
seeking an employment he **could** never find,
and on his return home in the evening sad

and depressed, he was obliged to tell falsehoods; to invent stories about an imaginary
sub-director, and a phantasmagoric office boy,
and to relate them all in a cheerful and
facetious manner. (I made use of this poor
fellow for the character of Père Joyeuse in
my novel the *Nabob*, who, in search of a
situation, also tells falsehoods to his
daughters.) I met him sometimes. It was
heartrending. His destitute condition decided me to try an appeal to Villemessant.
I thought, Villemessant can surely find him
some little corner in the *Figaro* office. But
it was impossible; every place was filled.
And then a communist! Fancy if it were
discovered that he, Villemessant, was employ-
ing a communist in his office! Nevertheless,
the story of the daughters, the white shirts,
the cravat bows, had, it seemed, softened the
heart of the good-natured ogre.

"Stop," he exclaimed; "how much did your
protégé receive a month?"

"Two hundred francs."

"Well then, I will remit to you two hundred francs a month for him until he finds a
situation. He will be able to keep up the

appearance of going to his office, his daughters will continue to tie his cravats." And he wound up his speech with his everlasting phrase, "What a good joke!"

It was indeed a capital joke; for three months the poor fellow continued to draw this little sum. At length he succeeded in finding a place, and he economized so steadily, and denied himself so vigorously, that one fine morning he brought me back the six hundred francs, and a beautiful letter of thanks for M. Villemessant, whose name I had revealed to him, and whom, notwithstanding the difference of their political views, he persisted in calling his benefactor. I carried it all to Villemessant.

"What a good joke! I gave him the money, and he wants to return it. This is the first time such a thing has happened to me. And a communard too; what a capital joke!"

Then followed exclamations, laughter, enthusiasm, and Villemessant, delighted, threw himself back in his arm-chair. But what ensued vividly paints the man. Happy and radiant, both on account of the kind action he had performed, and the natural pleasure felt, by even the most sceptical, on finding he has neither been duped nor yet obliged a thankless fellow, Villemessant, while talking, continued to pile up the six hundred francs, arranging them in six little heaps on the table. Suddenly, he turned towards me.

"I say, Daudet, there are five francs wanting!"

Five francs were indeed missing; one unfortunate tiny gold-piece had been forgotten in the lining of my pocket. In the midst of his enthusiasm, the man of business cropped up. Such is the complex character of this man, who, in reality, reflective, and very shrewd, hides these qualities under an appearance of impulsive good nature which would almost persuade one to believe that the poles could meet, that Toulouse is close to Blois, and that the turrets of Chambord are reflected in the waters of the Garonne.

In public as well as in private life, Villemessant had set up familiarity as a principle to be exercised towards others— be it understood—for he exacted great respect directly he himself was concerned. On the morrow of one of those biting articles, which he was in the habit of adding to the paper at the very last moment, when it was actually going to press, Villemessant was summoned to the Presidency of the *Corps legislatif* (this was under the Empire). If I am not mistaken, it was *à propos* of the famous article, '*Morny est dans l'affaire*' (Morny is implicated) which most old Boulevardiers will remember. The Duke was, or pretended to be, very angry, but our friend from Blois was not to be disconcerted.

"What, Monsieur le Duc, is it possible you have not sent for me to decorate me! The orderly you sent, with his large sealed envelope and his helmet, may boast that he gave me a famous thrill of emotion. My staff are already thinking of illuminations. This time it is a good joke!" And then he quickly poured forth stories, anecdotes and repartees without end, all thoroughly Parisian, accompanied by a hearty laugh, then a pretended air of concern, and a real and visible pleasure in repeating—"Monsieur le Duc!" and so the grievance was forgiven.

Elsewhere, at de Persigny's, for instance,

his familiarity did not meet with such success, and Villemessant one day found his facetious buffoonery, frozen by the chilly official atmosphere, fall flat and pointless. But Morny delighted in him, and forgave him everything. Thanks to his sovereign protection, the *Figaro* was able to play a thousand freaks. Then, too, what respect, what veneration they had for the President. I knew the time when they would have been capable of building a little chapel in the thickness of the walls of the editorial office, as to a protecting deity, a kind of Lares. However, all this did not prevent the *Figaro* from publishing one morning, in a most conspicuous place, *à propos* of a theatrical piece of M. de Saint Remy (the name with which the Duke signed his literary efforts), an article written by Henri Rochefort, as corrosive and biting as any acid, painful and irritating as a hundred needles forgotten in an arm-chair.

"What spite has this Rochefort against me? I have never done him any harm!" said the Duke with that artless vanity from which even the wiliest of statesmen are not always exempt, once they have put pen to paper;

and Villemessant putting on a contrite air, exclaimed,

"This is shocking ! Had I been there, such an article would never have been allowed to go to press. **You see how** grieved I am. But that **day—as** luck would have it—I never went near the office. The scoundrels have taken advantage of **my** absence. **I** never even saw the proofs."

The Duke might think what he pleased **of this** apology, but the article made a sensation. People eagerly read it, and bought it. Villemessant **did** not wish for anything better.

It is easy to see by the above anecdote **(and this was the basis of** the unity of this nature, **in appearance so diverse** and contradictory,) **that** Villemessant was above all devoted, **body and soul,** to his paper. After the first **cautious experiments** of *début*, after a few broadsides, fired somewhat **at** haphazard, **hither and** thither, after trying every point of the compass, once **the** right road found, **he travelled** undeviatingly along **it,** never for a moment allowing himself to be diverted **from his course.** His newspaper had become his life.

The man and his work resembled each
other, and no one, it may well be said, was
ever more exactly fitted for the measure of
his destiny.   Wonderfully active, energetic,
restless, overwhelming others by his huge
presence ; temperate too, as was then the

fashion (incredible as this may appear to the
present generation) ; never drinking, nor
smoking, fearing neither arguments, blows,
nor adventures, unscrupulous at heart, always
ready to throw overboard any prejudices, and
never having had any sincere political creed,

he was yet fond of displaying a Platonic and respectable legitimist attachment, as being that which he considered the best style. Villemessant was indeed the captain fitted to command the daring pirate craft, which for twenty years, under cover of the royal lily-sprinkled flag, sailed chiefly on its own account.

He was tyrannical and capricious, but beneath the surface it was the interest of his paper which always ruled the why and wherefore of this tyranny and caprice. In the year of grace 1858, we may see him at the Café des Variétés, or the Café Véron, on a Thursday morning at about eleven o'clock. The *Figaro* has just appeared. Villemessant is breakfasting. He gossips, relates anecdotes, which he will introduce into the next issue if they are laughed at; and will forget immediately, if they fall flat. He listens, and asks questions. "What do you think of So and So's article?—Charming.—Clever, is it not?—Wonderfully talented!" Villemessant returns beaming to the office. "Where is So and So? Tell him to come to me! Wonderfully talented! There is no one like him! All Paris is talking of his article."

And then *So and So* is congratulated, made much of, and his salary raised. Four days later, at the same table the same guest pronounces the same *So and So's* article to be tedious, and Villemessant hurries up again to the office, no longer beaming, but furiously angry ; and this time, instead of increasing the pay, settles and closes the account.

No doubt it was one of these post-prandial consultations that brought about the scene between Villemessant and Paul d'Ivoy, which so scandalized my youthful ingenuousness.

A writer more or less mattered little to Villemessant !

When one was dismissed, another was easily found, and the latest comer was always the best. According to him every one has an embryo article lying dormant in his brain, and the only question is what shall call it forth. Monselet has founded upon this a delightful story. " Villemessant meets a chimney-sweep in the street, carries him off to the office of the *Figaro*, has him washed, sets him down before some paper, and says to him ' Write ' ! The sweep writes, and the article is thought charming." 'Tis thus that

"All Paris" that can wield the pen, whether famous or unknown, has moved across the pages of the *Figaro*. In this manner many a worthy fellow, finding renewed in his favour, the history of the Quatrain of St. Aulaire, has had, owing to a happy inspiration of some fifteen lines, his brief moment of celebrity. If the miracle was not repeated, these ephemeral writers were pronounced "used up"! and "used-up" by Villemessant. I have known Paris quite filled with the battalions of the used-up. Ingenuous epoch! when fifteen lines was supposed to have "used one up."

Not that Villemessant despised literature, on the contrary! Only slightly educated himself, he felt for those who wrote well, and with command of language (it is one of his own expressions), the respect the peasant feels for the Latin of his priest. But he also felt instinctively, and not without reason, that these matters of style pertained more to the higher flights of literature. To supply his needs, the lightest French pastry was better suited than such heavy nourishment. He said one day to Jouvin, before me, with the

cynical frankness which was only excused
by his bluntness,

"You polish your writings; they are those of
a well read man; every one says so.   Clever,
learned, admirably well written, and I print
them.   Well, in my paper, no one reads them."

"No one reads them, indeed!"

"Will you make a bet? Daudet is here,
and can be witness.   I will print Cambronne's
famous word in the very middle of one of
your choicest pieces, and I will lose the bet
if any one finds it out!"

Truth compels me to say that Jouvin did
not care to risk the bet.

MY FIRST DRESS COAT.

How did I come by it, that first dress coat?
What primitive tailor, what confiding tradesman was it, trustful as Don Juan's famous
Monsieur Dimanche, who upon the faith of
my fantastic promises, decided one fine
morning on bringing it to me, brand new, and
artistically pinned up in a square of shiny
green calico? It would be difficult for me
to tell. Of the honest tailor, I can indeed
recall nothing—so many tailors have since

then crossed my **path—save** perhaps a vision
as in a luminous mist, of a thoughtful brow
and a large moustache. **The coat indeed**
is there, before my eyes. Its **image after**
twenty **years still** remains indelibly **graven on**
my memory, as on imperishable brass. **What**
a collar, my young friends! What lappels!
And, above all, what **skirts, shaped as the**
slimmest tail of the swallow! **My brother, a**
man of experience, had said: "**One must**
have a dress coat if one wishes to make one's
way in the world." And the dear fellow
counted much upon this piece of frippery **for**
the advancement **of my** fame and fortune.

This, my first **dress** coat, made **its**
début at Augustine Brohan's, **and** under
what circumstances worthy of being trans-
mitted to posterity, you shall now hear.

My little volume had just made its appearance, fresh and virginal, **in rose-tinted cover.**
A few critics had noticed my rhymes. **Even**
l'Official had printed **my name.** I was a
poet; **no** longer hidden **in a garret,** but
printed, published **and** exposed for sale in
the shop windows. I was astonished that
the busy folk in the streets did not turn

round to look at me, as my eighteen years
wandered along the pavement. I positively
felt upon my forehead the pleasant pressure
of a paper crown, made up of flattering
paragraphs culled from the papers.

One day some one proposed to get me an
invitation to Augustine Brohan's soirees.
Who ? some one. Some one, egad ! You
know him already : that eternal some one,
who is like every one else, that amiable
institution of Providence, who, of no personal
value in himself and a mere aquaintance in
the houses he frequents, yet goes everywhere,
introduces you everywhere, is the friend of a
day, of an hour, of whose name even you are
ignorant, that essentially Parisian type.

You may imagine with what enthusiasm I
accepted the proposal ! To be invited to
Augustine's house ! Augustine, the famous
actress, Augustine, the laughing representative
of Molière's comic muse, softened somewhat
by the more modern poetic smile of Musset's
genius ;—for while she acted the waiting
maids at the Theatre Français, Musset had
written his comedy *Louison* at her house ;
Augustine Brohan in short, in whom all

Paris delighted, vaunting her wit, quoting her repartees; and who might already be said to have adorned herself with that swallow's plume, unsullied yet by ink, but already well sharpened, with which she was hereafter to sign those charming *Lettres de Suzanne!*

"Lucky dog!" said my brother, helping me on with the coat; "your fortune is made."

Nine o'clock was striking as I sallied forth.

At that time Augustine Brohan was living in the rue Lord Byron, at the top of the Champs Elysées, in one of those pretty coquettish little houses which seem to ignorant provincials the realization of the poetical dreams which they weave for themselves from the pages of the novelist. A railing, a tiny garden, four steps covered by an awning, an entrance hall filled with flowers, and then opening immediately from it, the drawing-room, a brilliantly lighted room in

green, which I can see now vividly before
me.

How I managed to get up those steps, how
I made my entry, and how I presented myself, I cannot now remember. A footman
announced my name, but this name, which

he mumbled, produced no effect on the
brilliant assembly.   I can only recollect hearing a woman's voice say: "So much the
better, here is another dancer." It appears
they were short of dancers; but what an
entry for a poet !

Startled and humiliated, I tried to lose myself among the crowd. How can I describe
my dismay, when, a moment later, another
mistake arose? My long hair, my dark
and sombre looks excited general curiosity.
I heard them whispering near me : "Who is
it? Do look," and they laughed. At last
some one said,

"It is the Wallachian Prince !"

"The Wallachian Prince? Oh yes, very
likely."

I suppose that a Wallachian Prince had
been expected that evening. My rank being
thus settled for me, I was left in peace. But
for all that, you cannot imagine how heavily
my usurped crown weighed upon me all that
evening. First a dancing man! then a
Wallachian Prince! Could not these good
people see my lyre?

Fortunately for me, a startling piece of news,
flying from mouth to mouth, spread rapidly
through the ballroom, casting into oblivion
both the dancer and the Wallachian Prince.
Marriage was at that time much the fashion
among the feminine portion of the Comédie
Company, and it was generally at Augustine

Brohans' Wednesday receptions, where all the choicest talents of journalism, together **with** bankers and high government officials gathered round the lovely members or associates of the **Français,** that the foundations were laid of most of these romantic unions.

Mdlle. **Fix, the** witty actress, with her long **Hebrew** eyes, was soon to marry a great financier **and die** in childbirth. Mdlle. Figeac, Catholic and romantic, was already **dreaming** · **of the future day when** a priest would solemnly **bless her immense shop** on the Boulevard Haussmann, **just as if it were a vessel about to be launched.** Emilie Dubois, the fair Emilie **herself, although** destined by the delicate style **of her beauty to the** perpetual representation **of artless** maidens, had visions of orange **blossoms from** behind the protecting **shelter of her mother's** shawl. **As for** Madeleine **Brohan, the** handsome **and** majestic sister of Augustine, she was not marry-**ing. but was** unmarrying just **then ; thereby** giving Mario **Uchard** time **and money to devote** himself **to the four acts** of his *Fiammina*. **What an** explosion was therefore **caused in that circle so highly charged with**

matrimonial electricity, when this news
spread: "Gustave Fould has married
Valérie." Gustave Fould, the minister's
son! Valérie the charming actress! Now,
all this seems very far off. After a
flight to England, after letters in the papers
and pamphlets written, after waging a war in
Mirabeau's style against a father as inexor-
able as the "people's friend;" after the most
romantic of romances, ending up in the most
prosaic fashion, Gustave Fould, following, in
that, Mario Uchard's example, wrote the
Comtesse Romani, and eloquently displayed
the history of his misfortunes on the stage.
Mdlle. Valérie laid aside her married name,
and signed, under the pseudonym of Gustave
Haller, volumes entitled *Vertu*, with a lovely
picture on the palest of blue covers. So
the passionate language of love calmed down
in an ocean of literature! But what endless
gossip, what emotion it created that evening
in Augustine's green drawing-room! The
men, the officials, shook their heads, and with
mouths round with astonishment, said,
"Oh! This is very serious, very
serious!" One overheard the following

broken sentences. "Everything is going to
the dogs." "Respect has died out."
"The Emperor ought to interfere." "Sacred
rights." "Paternal authority." The women
on their side openly and gaily stood up in
defence of the two lovers who had fled to
London. "Well, if they are fond of each
other!" "Why should not the father
consent?" "He is a minister, but what
of that?" "Since the Revolution, thank
God, there is no longer a Bastille or a Fort-
l'Evêque!" Picture to yourself all these
people talking at the same time, and rising
brilliant above the noisy hubbub, like a
thread of gold on a piece of embroidery, the
clear ringing laugh of Augustine, her full
prominent eyes (those pretty short-sighted
eyes) gleaming with fun, and the whole of her
little plump figure the very embodiment of
mirth.

At last comparative calm was restored and
the quadrilles began. I danced. I was
obliged to do so! I danced moreover somewhat badly for a Wallachian Prince. The
quadrille once ended, I became stationary;
foolishly held back by my short sight—too

shy to sport an eyeglass, too much of a poet
to wear spectacles, and dreading lest, at the
slightest movement, I should bruise my knee
against the corner of some piece of furniture,
or plunge my nose into the trimming of a
bodice. Soon hunger and thirst interfered
in the matter; but for a kingdom I should
never have dared to approach the buffet with
all the rest of the world. I anxiously watched
for the moment when it should be deserted;
and while waiting, I joined the groups of
political talkers, assuming a serious air, and
feigning to scorn the charms of the smaller
salon, whence came to me, with the pleasant
sound of laughter and the tinkling of teaspoons
against the porcelain, a delicate aroma of
scented tea, of Spanish wines and cakes. At
last they came back to dance, and I gathered
up my courage. I entered, I was alone.

What a dazzling sight was that buffet! A
crystal pyramid under the blaze of the candles,
brilliant with glasses and decanters, white and
glittering as snow in sunshine! I took up a
glass as fragile as a flower, careful not to hold
it too tightly lest I should break the stem.
What should I pour into it? Come now,

courage, I say to myself, since no one can see
me.   I stretched out my hand, and took at
haphazard a decanter.   It must be kirsch, I
thought, from its diamond clearness.   Well,
I'll try a glass of kirsch; I like its perfume,
its bitter and wild perfume that reminds me
of the forest!   And so, like an epicure, I
slowly poured out, drop by drop, the
beautiful clear liquid.   I raised
the glass to my lips.   Oh,
horror! it was only water.   What
a grimace I made!   Suddenly
a duet of laughter resounded
from a black coat and a pink
dress that I had not perceived
flirting in a corner, and who
were amused at my mistake.
I endeavoured to replace my glass, but
I was nervous, my hand shook, and my sleeve
caught I know not what.   One glass, two
glasses, three glasses fell! I turned round, my
wretched coat tails swept a wild circle, and
the white pyramid crashed to the ground,
with all the sparkling, splintering, flashing
uproar of an iceberg breaking to pieces.
At the noise of the catastrophe the mistress

of the house rushes up. Luckily, she is as short-sighted as the Wallachian Prince, and he is able to escape from the buffet without being recognized. All the same, my evening

is spoilt. The massacre of small glasses and decanters weighs on my mind like a crime. My one idea is to get away. But the Dubois mamma, dazzled by my principality, catches hold of me, and **will not** allow me to leave till I have danced with her daughter, or indeed **with** both her daughters. I excuse myself as **best I** can ; I escape from her, and am stealing **away,** when **a** tall old man, with a shrewd smile, stopped **my** egress. **It is Doctor Ricord,** with **whom I** had **exchanged a few** words previously and **who** like the others, **takes** me for the Wallachian. "But, Prince, as you are inhabiting the Hôtel du Sénat, and as **we** are near neighbours, pray wait **for** me, I **can** offer you a seat **in my carriage."** How willingly would **I accept, but I have** no overcoat. What would **Ricord** think of a Wallachian Prince **without furs,** and shivering in his **dress** coat ? **Let me escape** quickly, and **hurry** home on foot, through **the snow and fog,** sooner than **allow my** poverty **to be seen.** Always **half blind and more confused** than ever, **I reach the door and slip out, not however** without **getting somehow entangled in** the tapestries. "Won't Monsieur **take his** coat ? " a footman calls after me.

There I was, at two o'clock in the morning, far from my home, alone in the streets, hungry and frozen, with the devil's own self, a badly

lined purse, in my pocket. But hunger
inspired me with a brilliant idea : "Suppose
I go to the markets !" I had often heard of
the markets, and of a certain Gaidras, whose
establishment remained open all night, and
where for the sum of three sous they provided
a plateful of succulent cabbage soup. By
Jove, yes, to the markets I would go. I
would sit down at those tables like the veriest
prowling vagabond. All my pride had vanished. The wind is icy cold ; hunger makes
me desperate. " My kingdom for a horse,"
said another prince, and I say to myself as I
trot along : " My principality, my Wallachian
principality, for a basin of good soup in a
warm corner.

Gaidras' establishment looks a mere filthy
hovel, all slimy and badly lighted, thrust back
beneath the colonnades of the old market
place. Often and often since then, when
noctambulism was the fashion, have we future
great men spent whole nights there, elbows
on table, amidst tobacco smoke and literary
talk. But at first I must own, notwithstanding
my hunger, I almost drew back at the sight
of those blackened dingy walls, that dense

smoke, those late sitters, snoring with their
backs against the wall or lapping up their soup
like dogs ; the amazing caps of the Don Juans
of the gutter, the enormous drab felt hats of

the market porters, and the healthy rough
blouse of the market gardener side by side
with the greasy tatters of the prowler of the
night. Nevertheless I entered, and I may at
once add that my black coat found its fellows.

Black coats that own no great coat are not
rare in Paris after midnight in the winter, and
they are hungry enough to eat three sous'

worth of cabbage soup! The cabbage soup
was however exquisite; full of perfume as a
garden, and smoking like a crater. I had two
helpings, although a custom peculiar to the

establishment—inspired by a wholesome
distrust—of fastening the forks and spoons
with a chain to the table, hindered me a little.
I paid, and fortified by the substantial mess,
resumed my way to the Quartier Latin.

What a picture that return home! The
return of the poet, trotting up the rue de
Tournon, with his coat collar turned up,
while dancing before his sleepy eyes are the
elegant shadows of a fashionable evening
party mingling with the famished spectres of
the market-place. He stands knocking his
boots against the kerbstone of the Hôtel du
Sénat, to shake off the snow, while opposite,
the bright lamps of a brougham light up the
front of an old mansion, and Doctor Ricord's
coachman cries out : "Gate, if you please."
Life in Paris is made up of these contrasts.

"A wasted evening!" said my brother, the
next morning. "You have been taken for a
Wallachian Prince, and have not succeeded
in launching your book. But all is not yet
lost; you must make up for it when you
make your 'digestion call!' as we say in
Paris."

The digestion of a glass of water, what.

irony! It was quite two months before I made up my mind to pay that call. However one day I summoned up courage. Besides her official receptions on Wednesdays, Augustine Brohan received more unceremoniously on Sunday afternoon. I resolutely started off.

In Paris a *matinée* that respects itself cannot decently begin till three or even four o'clock in the afternoon. I, poor unsophisticated mortal, taking the word *matinée* literally, arrived there at one o'clock, and thought myself already late.

"How early you come, sir!" said a fair-haired little boy of five or six years of age, who, dressed in an embroidered velvet suit, was riding a mechanical toy horse through the fresh spring greenery of the garden. The young man impressed me! I bowed to the fair curls, the horse, the velvet, the embroideries, and too bashful to retrace my steps, I went in. Madame was not yet dressed, and I waited all alone for half an hour. At last Madame made her appearance; screwing up her eyes she recognized her Wallachian Prince; then by way of beginning the

conversation, **she** said : " You are not at
La Marche, Prince?" **At** *La Marche*, I,
who had never seen a race nor a jockey!

Really I felt too much ashamed! a sudden
throb rose from my heart to my brain ; and
then the bright sun, **the** sweet perfume of
spring wafted from the garden through the
open casement, the absence of all ceremony,
the smiling and kind-hearted little woman, all
combined to encourage me, and **I** poured
forth my whole heart. I told her all—con-
fessing everything: how I was neither a
Wallachian, nor **a** Prince, but a simple poet ;
and the adventure of my glass of **kirsch, and**
my supper at the markets, and my wretched
return home, and my provincial timidity, and
my short sight, and my aspirations—all seasoned by the accent of my southern province.
Augustine Brohan laughed heartily. Sud-
denly a bell rang.

"Ah ! my dragoons," she exclaimed.

"What dragoons ? "

"Two dragoons they are sending me from
the camp at Châlons, **and** who, it appears,
have a wonderful taste for acting."

I wished to take leave.

" No, no, stay ; we are going to rehearse
Lait d'ânesse, and you shall help me with
your criticisms. Sit down by me on the
sofa ! "

Two huge fellows came in, shy, awkward,
tightly belted, purple in the face (one of them
acts somewhere at the present day). A fold-
ing screen is arranged, I settle myself, and the
representation begins.

" They do not act so badly," said Augustine
Brohan in a low tone, " but what boots ! My
dear critic, do you smell those boots ? "

To be on these intimate terms with the
wittiest actress in Paris raised me to the
seventh heaven. I threw myself back on the
sofa, nodding my head and smiling in a capable manner. I was positively intoxicated
with delight.

Even now I can recall the smallest details
of that interview. But see how all depends
upon our point of view. I had told Sarcey
the comical story of my first appearance in
society, and one day Sarcey repeated it to
Augustine Brohan. Well the ungrateful
Augustine—whom, it is true, I have not seen
for thirty years—swore most sincerely that

D

she knew nothing of me but my books. She
had forgotten everything! Everything—all
that had played such an important part in my
life—the broken glasses, the Wallachian Prince,
the rehearsal of *Lait d'ânesse,* and the boots
of the heavy dragoons.

THE STORY OF MY BOOKS.

"LE PETIT CHOSE."

(" *Little What's His Name.*")

No other book of mine has ever been written under such capricious and varying conditions. Without plan or notes, it was a frenzied, hurried improvisation dashed down on coarse whitey-brown paper, on which my pen stumbled as it raced along, and which, once

scribbled over, I threw impetuously on to the
floor.   All this took place some two hundred
leagues from Paris, between Beaucaire and
Nismes, in a large, lonely, far-away country
house, that some relatives had kindly placed

at my disposal during the few winter months
I had come thither in search of the closing
scenes of a drama that I could by no means
bring satisfactorily to its climax; but the
melancholy quiet of the great plains, the

groves of mulberry and olive trees, and the
vines undulating down to the Rhone, in short,
the gloom of this retreat in the midst of nature
was out of harmony with the conventional
forms of a theatrical composition.   Probably

also, the country air, the mistral sweeping
across the sun, the neighbourhood of the
town where I was born, the names of the little
villages, where as a boy, I used to play,
Bezouces, Redessan, Jonquières, stirred up
within me, a whole world of old memories,

and soon I abandoned my drama, in order to write a kind of autobiography—*Le Petit Chose*—the story of a child.

Begun during the first days of February, 1866, this headlong work was carried on without a break till the second fortnight in March. Nowhere else, at no other time of my life, not even when a caprice for silence and solitude led me to shut myself up in a lighthouse, have I lived so completely isolated. The house was far from the road, surrounded by fields; apart even from the farm belonging to it, the noises of which never reached me. Twice in the day, the wife of the *baïlo* (farmer) spread my meal, at the end of a vast dining-room, all the windows of which, with one exception, had closed shutters. This stuttering Provençale, dark complexioned, with a nose flattened like that of a Kafir, could not make out what strange task had sent me into the country in midwinter, and held me in suspicious terror, setting down the dishes in haste, leaving me without uttering a word, avoiding even a glance in my direction. It was the only face I saw during that hermit-like existence, the monotony of which was only broken by a

stroll in the evening through the avenue of
tall plane trees, standing bare amid the plaintive sighing of the wind, and the sadness of
the cold red winter sunset, which, rapidly
fading, was greeted by a discordant clamour
of frogs. Directly I had finished my book, I
set to work on that laborious business, the
second copy. It was contrary to my whole
nature of Improvisatore, of Troubadour : and
I was attacking it with all my courage, when
one morning, the voice of the *baïlesse*, hailed
me loudly in the local dialect : "*Moussu,
moussu, vaqui un homo!*"—Sir, sir, here is
a man !"—The man was a Parisian, a
newspaper reporter, sent down to some
agricultural show near there, and who, knowing I was somewhere in the neighbourhood,
came to see me. He breakfasted with me ;
we gossipped about the news, the papers, the
boulevards. The Paris fever seized me, and
in the evening I started off with my intruding
guest.

This abrupt relinquishment of my labour,
the suddenness with which I forsook my
work, just as it was taking form, gives an
exact idea of my life at that time, influenced

by every passing fancy, full **of** fitful **impulse,**
whim more than will, following only **the**
caprice of the moment, and the **blind fancy**
of **a** youth that threatened to **be** endless.
On my return to Paris, I left my manuscript
to grow yellow for many **a day** at the bottom
of a drawer, not being **able to find** in **my**
broken-up existence, **the necessary** time for
a more lengthy task ; but the following
winter, pursued by the thought of this book,
I took the violent resolution of withdrawing
myself from everything that could possibly
divert me from **my** work,—from **the** noisy
irruptions, which **at** that time, turned my
defenceless dwelling **into a regular** gipsy
camp, **and I** settled **myself in a** friend's
apartment—**in** that small room which Jean
Duboys then occupied on **the** entresol of the
Hôtel **Lassus,** Place de l'Odéon.

Jean Duboys, to whom his plays and novels
lent **a** certain **celebrity,** was **a kind,** good
creature, gentle and timid, with the confiding
smile of a child beaming over **a** Robinson
Crusoe style **of beard, a hirsute, unkempt**
beard **that did not seem to belong to his
face.** His **writing was** wanting in style, **but I**

appreciated his good-nature, I admired the courage with which he devoted himself to interminably long novels, arranged beforehand in given lengths, of which he wrote each day so many words, lines and pages. At last a play of his entitled : *La Volonté*, was produced at the Comédie Française, and although set forth in execrable verse, I, who was so devoid of will myself, was impressed by it. I had therefore come to place myself under his influence, hoping to gain a love of work from the constant example of this indefatigable toiler.

The fact is that for two or three months I fagged away, seated at a little table next to his, under the light of a low arched window, which framed, as in a picture, the Odéon and its portico, and the deserted square, all glittering with hoar frost. From time to time Duboys, who was working at a great sensational novel, would interrupt himself to relate to me the combination of incidents in his book, or to develop his theories on the evolution of the human species. In the mind of this methodical and quiet bureaucrat there ran a vein of visionary mysticism, just

as, in his library, there was a shelf devoted
to the Kabbalah, the black arts, the most
whimsical lucubrations. Later on, the flaw
in his brain deepened, insanity ensued, and
poor Jean Duboys died mad at the close of
the siege, without having finished his great
philosophical poem *Enceldonne*, **wherein**
all humanity was **to revolve** around a central
axis. But who then, would have suspected
the sad destiny of **this** excellent fellow, **so**
quiet and sensible, whom I watched enviously,
while he covered **with his neat** writing, page
after **page of a novel for some** trumpery
paper, looking up **now and then at the clock,**
in order to ascertain **if he had finished** his
task. ?

There was a hard **frost that** winter, and,
notwithstanding the **scuttles** full of coal
swallowed up by the grate, we often saw, during those laborious night vigils so indefinitely
prolonged, the rime throwing over the window
panes a veil of fantastic tracery. Outside,
chill shadows wandered through the opaque
mist that filled the square : it was the audience
leaving the Odéon, or the students who were
making their way to Bullier, shouting as they

went along, in the exuberance of their spirits.
On the evenings of the masked balls, the
narrow stairs of the hotel shook beneath the
mad rushes of hurrying footsteps, accompanied by the constant tinkle of the jester's
bells.   Far on in the night the same fool's
cap and bells pursued its mad career of folly
on its homeward road, and often, when the
hotel waiters, sleeping too soundly, were slow
to open, I heard the ringing of the little bells
before the door diminishing in force as the
wearer became disheartened, and reminding
me of Edgar Poe's *Cask of Amontillado,*
where the unhappy walled-up wretch, weary
of supplication and screaming, only betrays
his presence by the last convulsive movement
of his fool's cap. I still retain a delightful
remembrance of the winter evenings during
which I wrote the first part of *Le Petit
Chose.* The second part was written very
much later. In the interval between the two
parts an unexpected, serious and decisive
event took place. I married ! How did
that happen ? To what magic art did such
a wild gipsy as I was then fall a victim ?
What spell was cast over me ? What charm

was strong enough to bind fast my once ever-
changing caprice?

For several months the manuscript was
again abandoned, forgotten at the bottom of
a wedding trunk, spread out on hotel tables
in front of an arid ink-stand and a dried-up
pen. It was so delicious under the pine
trees of the Estérel; it was so pleasant to fish
for sea-urchins off the rocks of Pormieu!
Then settling the little household, and the
novelty of home life, the nest to be built
and adorned, all were excellent pretexts for
idleness.

It was only the following summer, under
the shadow of the big trees of the Château
de Vigneux, whose flat Italian roofs and
tall shrubberies extend towards the plains of
Villeneuve-Saint-Georges, that I resumed my
interminable novel. Six exquisite months,
far from Paris—at that time thrown into
confusion by the Exhibition (which I refused
even to look at) of 1867.

I wrote *Le Petit Chose* sometimes
seated on a mossy bank at the end of the
park, where the gambols of the rabbits and
the gliding of the adders through the heather

alone disturbed me: or in the boat on the pond, which shimmered with every colour of the prism, reflected from the glory of the summer sky ; or else, on the rainy days, in our room, while my wife played Chopin to me, music that I cannot even now listen to without recalling the dripping of the rain- drops on the green sea of elm trees, the harsh scream of the pea- cocks, the call of the pheasant, mingled with the perfume of the trees in flower and the smell of the damp woods.

At last, in autumn, the book was finished, appeared first in numbers, in Paul Dalloz's *Petit Moniteur*, was afterwards published by Hetzel, and met with some success, notwithstanding all its defects.

I have mentioned in what manner this first work of **any** length had been undertaken, thoughtlessly, and at random ; but its most serious fault was, that I wrote it too soon. One **is not** sufficently **matured** at five and twenty, **to be** able **to** look back upon, and annotate **one's** own life : **and** *Le Petit Chose,* especially **the first part,** is in reality, but an echo of **my own childhood and youth.**

Later **on, I** should **have** had less fear of dwelling too much upon childish trifles, and I should have given fuller play to the distant recollections in which lie those first impressions which are so vivid and so deep, **that all that comes after,** renews but never surpasses them.   **In the** ever-increasing movement **of life, in the** perpetual flow of days and **years, facts are lost,** fade away and disappear, but **the past** stands out, clear and bright, bathed **in the** light **of the** breaking dawn.   We may forget a recent date, a face **seen** but **yesterday, but we** ever remember the **pattern on the walls of** our childhood's nursery, **and a name or a** lullaby of the time **when we could not read.   How far back can** memory reach **into those past** times !   **I can**

remember, for instance, when I was three
years old, a display of fireworks at Nismes,
given in honour of some Saint Louis or
another, and which I saw, carried in arms,
from a hill top covered with pines. The
minutest details are even now present to my
mind—the sighing of the night wind, no
doubt my first night in the open air, the
noisy delight of the crowd, the "ah!" rising
and swelling, bursting forth with each fresh
rocket, and the catherine wheels shedding a
pallid and spectral light on the faces around
me.

Again, I see myself about the same time,
standing on a chair in the small clerical school
in front of a blackboard, chalking my A B C,
all proud of my precocious knowledge. What
memories, and sensations, what sounds and
perfumes come back from those past days
as from another world, and yet among them
all, not the trace of an incident or an
emotion !

At the further end of the manufactory
where *Petit Chose* spent his childhood, near
some forsaken buildings, the doors of which
beat to and fro in the solitary wind, there grew,

out of doors, some **tall** pink oleanders, dif-
fusing around them **a** bitter-sweet scent,
which haunts me still, even after forty years.
I should wish for **a little** more of that same
scent in the first pages of my book.

Too brief also, are the chapters on Lyons,
where I have neglected many vivid and valu-
able sensations. **Not that my** childish eyes
could have comprehended the originality and
grandeur of that industrial **and mystical town,**
with **the** ever-present mists **rising from its
rivers,** penetrating its walls and its people,
and permeating **even** the works **of** its writers
and artists:—**Ballanche,** Flandrin, de Laprade,
Chenavard, Puvis de Chavannes.   But if the
inner personality of the country escaped me,
I have, **on the other** hand, imperishable
memories, **all of** which found their place in
Le Petit Chose, **of** the enormous working hive
of the Croix-Rousse, buzzing with the sound
of its hundred thousand looms : and, on the
rising ground opposite, Fourvières, proces-
sions **streaming through its** narrow streets,
lined on each side with religious wares, and
stalls full of relics ; and resounding with con-
tinual pealing **and chiming.**

What I always find faithfully represented is the *ennui*, the feeling of exile, the sufferings of a southern family lost and enveloped in the foggy atmosphere of Lyons—that change from one province to another, the difference of climate, customs, language ; that mental distance, never entirely obliterated by facilities of communication. I was ten years of age, and already sometimes tormented by the desire to lose my own personality, to incarnate myself in other beings : the mania for observation and analysis was already laying hold of me. My chief amusement during my walks was to pick out some passer-by, to follow him through Lyons, through all his idle strolling or busy occupations, striving to identify myself with his life, and to enter into his innermost thoughts.

One day however, when I had thus followed a gorgeous female in brilliant attire to the door of a small house with closed shutters, from the ground-floor of which arose a sound of discordant voices, accompanied by the harp, my parents, to whom I expressed my surprise, forbade my wandering studies and observations of life.

But how came **I**, while recording the different stages of my youth, to pass by without a word the various religious crises which stirred Le Petit Chose so painfully : and the rebellion of his spirit against the irrational mysteries he was bound to believe—rebellions quickly followed by remorse **and despair,** prostrating **the** child on his knees in **dark** corners of lonely churches, into which he stole furtively, ashamed and trembling at the idea **of** being seen.   And moreover why did I leave the little man that appearance of gentle-**ness** and good temper, without mentioning the diabolic phase upon which he entered **towards** his thirteenth year, inspired **by a** sudden thirst for life **and** its enjoyments, an impatient desire to tear himself away from the withering sadness and tears that filled his parental home, rendered day by day more sombre by approaching ruin ?   It was the out-spring of **a southern** temperament, and an imagination too much restrained.   The delicate and timid child became transformed **into** a bold and violent spirit, ready for any **mad prank.**   He neglected school, and spent **his** days on **the river,** amongst the **crowd** of

steamboats, barges and tugs, rowing about in
the rain, a pipe between his teeth, a flask of
absinthe or brandy in his pocket, having endless hairbreadth escapes from the paddles of
a steamer, the collision of a collier, from the
swift current which bore him against the

piles of a bridge, or under a towing-rope, half
drowned, picked up again with broken head,
cuffed by the watermen, who were exasperated
by the awkwardness of this brat, too weak
for his oars ; and in the midst of all these
dangers, and blows, and fatigues, he felt a

savage delight, a widening of his whole being, and of the sombre horizon.   Later on, a few *Contes du Lundi* have given a sketch of these momentous days, but how much better would it have been placed in *L'Histoire d'un Enfant.*

The naughty little Chose already possessed a faculty that he has never lost—the gift of seeing and judging himself, of seizing himself in the very act, *in flagrante delicto*, as if he were perpetually accompanied by a ferocious and formidable overseer.   Not what is called conscience, for our conscience scolds, preaches, and, mixing itself up with our affairs, modifies or arrests them.   And then one can lull it to sleep, that good, kind conscience, with easy excuses or subterfuges ; whereas the witness of whom I am speaking never grew weaker, never mixed in one's life, and remained simply on the watch.   It was as an inner eye, impassible, rigid, a cold and inert *double*, who, during the most violent outbursts of Petit Chose, quietly observed everything, and not till next day said "A word with you." Read the chapter headed " He is dead ! pray for him !"   It is a leaf out of my life,

absolutely true. It was exactly thus that we
learnt my brother's death, and I can still hear
ringing in my ears the poor father's cry, guessing that his son was dead; so heartrending,
so piteous, that first great cry of human grief
near to me in every sense, that all night
long, weeping and despairing, I found myself repeating. "He is dead," with the paternal intonation. In this manner was my
double revealed to me; the implacable
witness, who in the midst of our mourning,
had noted, as at the theatre, the truth to
nature of that wail of anguish, and practised
it on my lips. I regret on reading over this
book to find nothing of this avowal, especially
in that first part, where the character of
Daniel Eyssette resembles me so much.

Yes, it is indeed myself, that little Chose,
obliged at sixteen years of age to gain his
daily bread at that horrible trade of usher,
and carrying it out far away in the provinces,
in a country of pits and furnaces, which sent
us rough little mountaineers, who insulted me
in the harsh and brutal dialect of the
Cévennes. A prey to all the persecutions
of these little monsters, surrounded by bigots,

and coarse vulgar pedants who despised me,
I there suffered all the degrading humiliations
of poverty.

No other sympathy had I, in the melancholy of that prison, but that of the priest,
whom I have called " *l'Abbé Germane*," and
the frightful little " *Bamban*," whose ludicrous
face, always covered with ink and mud,
rises up sadly before me while I write.

I remember yet another of my little pupils,
a delicate and refined nature, to whom I had
become much attached, and whose studies
I carefully encouraged, for the mere pleasure
of watching the development of his youthful
intelligence as one watches a bud opening in
the spring. Touched by the care I bestowed
upon him, the child had extracted a promise
that I should spend the holidays at his home
in the country. His parents would be so
happy to know me and thank me ! And, on
the day when the prizes were distributed,
after all his successes—for which he was
greatly indebted to me—my pupil came,
and taking me by the hand, prettily led me
up to his people ; father, mother and sisters,
all elegantly dressed, and busily occupied

putting his prizes into their waggonette. I must
have presented a somewhat dilapidated and
uninviting appearance in my shabby old
clothes, for the family hardly bestowed a
glance upon me, and the poor little fellow
went off with tears in his eyes, ashamed at
his own and my disappointment. Cruel and
humiliating moments, withering and dis-
honouring life ! I trembled with rage, in my
little attic under the roof, while the carriage
bore away the child, loaded with his wreaths,
and the vulgar folk who had wounded me in
such a contemptible manner.

How often, long after I had taken leave of
that prison house at Alais, did I not awake
in the middle of the night, bathed in tears,
dreaming that I was still there, a victimized
usher. Fortunately, this painful beginning of
life has not hardened me, and I do not curse
too roundly those wretched days, which
enabled me to bear more lightly the trials of
my literary novitiate and first struggling years
in Paris. Those were indeed hard times, of
which the story of little Chose gives but a
faint idea.

Moreover there is but little taken from

real life in the second part of the book, except my shoeless arrival, my blue socks, my goloshes, and the brotherly welcome, the ingenious devotion of that " *Mother Jacques,*" whose real name is Ernest Daudet, the one bright figure of my childhood, and my youth. But with this exception, all the other personages are purely fictitious.

Not however that models were wanting, some most interesting and rare, but as I have just said, I was too young when I wrote the book.　Part of my life was still too near to me, I wanted distance to focus it all, and not seeing, I invented.　For instance the little Chose has never been an actor, indeed he has never been able to say a word in public. He has never dealt in china : Pierrotte with her black eyes, the lady on the first floor, her negress ' *White Coucou* ' thrown on the canvas, as the painters say, are wanting both in depth and vitality.　The same may be said of the literary outlines, in which people have chosen to recognize wounding personalities that I never even dreamt of.

To be noted however among the realities of my book, is the description of the room

under the roof, near the steeple of Saint-
Germain-de-Prés, in a house since pulled
down, and whose absence makes a blank
before my eyes each time I pass by and look
up, seeking in vain for the place where so
much folly and so much misery, so many
nights of fruitful labour or of despairing
solitude were spent.

LITERARY SALONS.[1]

AT the present day, not one such, I believe, remains. We have other *salons*, more
in unison with the spirit of the time—political
salons—like those of Madame Edmond Adam,
or Madame d'Haussonville, either all of one
political party or all of the other, where pre-
fects are proposed, ministers deposed, and
where on gala days appear the Orléans
princes or Gambetta. Then there are the
salons where people amuse themselves, or
rather try to amuse themselves; full of re-

[1] Written in 1879 for the *Nouveau Temps*,
published at St. Petersburg.

membrances and regrets! They sup, they
play, they endeavour to the utmost of their
power to revive the delights of Compiègne;
pretty hothouses, beneath whose fragile crystal
roof bloom in all their factitious splendour, the
scentless flowers of the hollow worldly circles.
But the real literary *salon*, where, gathered
round a gracious and kindly muse, literary
men, or those who believed themselves such,
assembled once a week to recite their little
verses, dipping the while their little dry bis-
cuits in little cups of tea; a *salon* like this
in short, has undoubtedly disappeared. Although I am not old, it has yet been my lot
to know some of these blue-stocking *salons*,
banished nowadays to the provinces, more
out of fashion even than the guitar, the "aspirations after the Unknowable," and the
quatrains scribbled in ladies' albums.

Let us fan our recollections of twenty years
ago. *Pft! pft! pft!* The dust rises in a
dainty cloud, and in this cloud, distinctly
drawn and becoming gradually clearer, as the
apparition of a fairy, is the pleasing outline
of excellent Madame Ancelot. Madame
Ancelot lived at that time in the Rue Saint

Guillaume ; a short **street of** provincial aspect, forgotten somehow by the indefatigable
Haussmann in the very heart of Paris, where
the grass **grew between** the stones, where the
sound of wheels was never heard, and where
the tall houses, too tall in proportion for their
three stories, allowed **only** a distant and chilly
daylight to penetrate. The silent old man-
sion with **its great gate never** open, the
shutters of its balconies always closed, looked
as if it had lain for centuries asleep under the
wand of some enchanter. The interior did
not belie the promise of the exterior ; the
corridor was all in white, the staircase dark
and echoing, the ceilings lofty, and over the
great windows pictures **were** let into the
panelling. Everything was faded and wan,
having lost all **semblance** of vitality ; and in
the **middle of** it all, well **suited to her sur-**
roundings, **was Madame Ancelot all** in white,
round and wrinkled like a little red apple,
just such in fact, as one pictures to oneself
the fairies of the stories, who never die, but
grow gently old, through thousands of years.
Madame Ancelot loved birds like all good
fairies. **All round the** drawing-room, hiding

the walls, were piled cages of warblers, as at
the bird-fanciers' shops on the quay. But
even the birds themselves seemed to pipe
only old-fashioned tunes. In the place of
honour, in the best light and most prominent
position, hung a large portrait by Baron
Gérard, of the muse of this household, with
flowing locks, dressed in the fashion of Louis

the Eighteenth's time, smiling with the smile
then in vogue and posed in a well-chosen
attitude to set off, with a suggestion of flight,
like that of Galatea, the tip of an exquisitely
white and round shoulder. Forty years later
than the date of the picture of which I speak,
Madame Ancelot still wore low dresses, but
it must be owned, the shoulders displayed

were no longer those marvels of round white
loveliness formerly painted by Baron Gérard.
But what did the dear old lady care? In
1858 she still believed herself the beautiful
Madame Ancelot of 1823, when Paris was
applauding her pretty piece of *Marie; ou, les
Trois Époques!* There was nothing besides

to warn her of the flight of time; everything
aged and faded with herself, the roses of the
carpets, the cords and tassels of the hangings,
the human beings around her and the remembrances of other days; and while the
century marched on, this arrested existence,
this interior of another age, motionless as a

vessel at anchor, remained buried in the stillness of the silent past.

One simple word would have broken the spell! But who would pronounce that sacrilegious word? who would have the courage to say, "We are growing old?" The *habitués* least of all, for they too were of the same period, they too could not believe they were growing older. Behold M. Patin, the illustrious M. Patin, professor at the Sorbonne, playing the young man over there, in the left-hand corner by the window. He is a little man, with white hair smartly curled, and of a discreet friskiness suited to a pedant of the First Empire. Then there is Viennet, the Voltairian writer of fables, long and spare as the crane of his own dry fables. The divinity of the *salon*, admired and petted by all, surrounded by a crowd of worshippers, was Alfred de Vigny, great poet indeed, but great poet of yet another epoch, looking eccentric and obsolete with his angelic airs and scattered white locks, too long for his diminutive figure. Alfred de Vigny had, when dying, bequeathed his parrokeet to Madame Ancelot. The parrokeet, on a gilt perch, took the place of

honour in the middle of the room, and the
old *habitués* stuffed it with good things, for
was it not the parrot of de Vigny? Some
profane jesters nicknamed it "Eloa," on
account of its great beak and its profound
eye. But this was hereafter; at the time
when I was presented to Madame Ancelot,
the poet was still alive, and the parrot did
not yet mingle its short, shrill, and aged cry
with the formidable burst of song, which—as
a kind of protest, I imagine—rose from all
the cages whenever M. Viennet tried to
recite a few verses.

Sometimes a few younger people enlivened
the evening. On such days one might meet
Lachaud, the celebrated lawyer with his wife,
Madame Ancelot's daughter; she, somewhat
melancholy, he, fat and smooth, with a fine
Roman head, which might have been that of
a jurisconsult of the last days of Rome. There
were poets too, Octave Lacroix, the author of
the *Chanson d'Avril;* and *L'Amour et son
Train;* both of which were played at the Théâtre
Français; he impressed me strongly, for though
mild enough in appearance, he was secretary
to Sainte-Beuve. Emmanuel des Essarts was

there, brought by his father, a distinguished
writer and librarian at Sainte-Geneviève.
Emmanuel des Essarts was at that time quite
a young man, scarcely known, and wearing
still in his buttonhole, if I recollect aright, the
green badge of the " Ecole Normale." He

occupies at present the literary chair at the
University of Clermont, which does not prevent him from publishing, most years, one or
two volumes in which may be found some
charming verses. Delightful Professor, as you
may guess, with a twig of the poet's myrtle

E

wreath in his cap. Then there were the ladies, poetical ladies like Madame Anaïs Ségalas, and from time to time a newly discovered budding muse, with golden curls and blue eye full of inspiration, who attitudinized

in the antiquated style of Delphine Gay and Élisa Mercœur. Thus did the fair Jenny Sabatier one day make her appearance, her real name being Tirecuir—terribly prosaic name for a muse. From me also, verses were

expected, as from the others, but it appears I
was bashful, and that my voice was affected
thereby. "Louder," Madame Ancelot used
to say to me, "louder, M. de la Rochejacque-
lein cannot hear you!" There were half
a dozen such old fogies, deaf as Etruscan
vases, never hearing, but always assuming an
attentive air, with the left hand well rounded,
trumpet fashion behind the ear. Gustave
Nadaud however could make himself heard.
Stumpy, snub-nosed, a large face, an expansive
smile, and affecting a rustic cheerfulness which
was not without its merit in this sleepy
atmosphere, the author of *Les Deux Gen-
darmes* would take his seat at the piano, sing
loudly, thump hard and awaken everybody.
What a success he always had! We were all
jealous of him. Sometimes too, an actress,
anxious to make her way, would come to
declaim a few verses. It was a tradition of
the house that Rachel had recited stanzas in
Madame Ancelot's drawing-room; a picture
near the chimneypiece testified to the fact.
The recitation of stanzas continued; only it
was no longer Rachel who recited. This
picture was not the only one of its kind, one

might be found in nearly every corner—all the
work of Madame Ancelot, who had not dis-
dained to handle the brush and mahl stick in
her **time,** and all dedicated to her "Salon,"
intended to perpetuate the remembrance of
some great **event in her tiny** world. **The**
inquiring **mind will be** able to find **them**
reproduced (oh, cruel **irony of fate, by E.**
Benassit, the most sceptical of painters,) in a
kind of autobiography, *Mon Salon*, by Madame
Ancelot, published by Dentu. Each of the
"faithful" **is** therein portrayed, and I think
that even I am represented in it, somewhere
in the background.

This somewhat heterogeneous society met
thus every Tuesday, **rue** Saint Guillaume.
They came late, and for the following reason :
a few doors off, rue du Cherche-Midi, placed
there like a permanent protest, was a rival
"salon"; the salon of **Madame** Mélanie
Waldor. In former days the two muses had
been intimate, Madame Ancelot had even at
first given **Mélanie a** helping hand. Then
suddenly Mélanie had shaken her off, had
raised up altar against altar—a repetition of
the conduct of Mademoiselle de Lespinasse

and Madame du Deffand. Mélanie Waldor wrote—novels, verses, and a play called : *La Tirelire de Jeannette.* One day Alfred de Musset, in a fit of ill humour, wrote some terribly sarcastic lines about her, a biting and high flavoured medley, savouring of Aretino and Juvenal, which will, for want of a better reason, hand the name of the muse down to posterity on the wings of clandestine publications. What could Madame Waldor have done to the spoilt child? I remember her well, dressed all in velvet, with her black hair—black with the blackness of a centenarian raven that absolutely refuses to grow white— hanging loosely over the sofa, on which exhausted and languid she reclined, affecting broken-hearted attitudes. But the eye brightened and the lips became viperish directly ' *she* was mentioned. *She !* that is to say the other one, the enemy, good old Madame Ancelot. Between these two it was war to the knife. Madame Waldor had purposely chosen the same day, and when at about eleven o'clock one tried to slip away unobserved and dash over to the opposite house, a freezing glance nailed the truant to his

place. Escape was impossible, so one
remained; to make wit, to abuse poor old
Ancelot, and to exercise one's talents in repeating or inventing scandalous anecdotes.
Over the way one made up for it by telling a
thousand mysterious legends about Madame
Waldor's political influence.

What time lost, what hours wasted on those
venomous or stupid little nothings, in that atmosphere of little mouldy verses, and little
rancid calumnies, on those paste-board Parnassus, where no spring ever flowed, no bird
ever sang, and where the poetic laurel wreath
was the colour of the green leather cushion
of a head clerk's stool! To think that I too
have climbed those Parnassus! One must see
everything in youth! It lasted just as long as
my dress coat lasted.

Poor dear old coat, what narrow passages
did its tails not brush through in those days;
what banisters did it not polish with its
sleeves. I remember having worn it also in
the "salon" of the Comtesse Chodsko.

The Countess had for husband a kind,
learned old man, who was hardly ever seen,
and not of much account. She must have

been very handsome ; at this time she was
a tall, stiff, dry woman, with a domineering
and even ill-tempered air. Murger, it was
said, had been much struck by her, and
represented her in his *Madame Olympe.*

Murger had in truth at one time made a
voyage of discovery into that fashionable
society which he did not generally frequent,
and here was the society which he ingenuously believed himself to have discovered.

This fashionable society was meanly lodged, perched high up on a third floor of the rue de Tournon in three cold and shabby little rooms, looking out on a small courtyard. Nevertheless one went to them, and the company was not of the vulgar herd. It was there I saw for the first time, Philarète Chasles, whose restless spirit and nervous pen belonged to the school of Saint-Simon and Michelet. His astonishing *Mémoires*, full of fight and devilment, made up of attacks and parrying thrusts, seeming filled from the first chapter to the last with the continual noise of clashing foils and shivering swords, are now being published, and passing almost unnoticed through the midst of a Paris absolutely indifferent to anything that is not either painting or politics. Above all things a

literary man, he was, like Balzac, devoured all his life by the thirst for a wider existence and a love of dandyism ; he remained a librarian at the very gates of the *Académie*, which however were never opened to him, why, no one knows, and he died at Venice of cholera.

I also met there Pierre Véron, Philibert Audebrand, and a curious couple—very curious, and at the same time very sympathetic, whom I must crave leave to introduce to my reader. We are now in the drawing-room, let us seat ourselves and look on : the door opens, and Philoxène Boyer and his wife make their entry. Philoxène Boyer ! another of those strange sons, the terror and punishment of families, chance productions that no atavism can account for ; seeds brought from we know not whence on the wings of the wind, from far away over the seas ; and which one fine day with their curiously jagged leaves and their strangely vivid flowers, suddenly burst forth into bloom in the midst of a cabbage plot, in the very middle of a quiet *bourgeois* kitchen garden ! Son of Boyer, he who knew more Greek

than any **other** man **of** his time : **born**
between **two** pages of a lexicon, never
having as **a** child known any other walk
or garden than the learned garden of Greek
roots, fed **upon** Greek, anointed with Greek ;
Philoxène **with** his Greek nomenclature
seemed destined to **see his name graven**
on the marble, side by side with **those of**
the Eggers and the Estiennes in the pantheon
of the Hellenists. But Father Boyer counted
without **Balzac.** Philoxène, like all school-
boys of **that date,** kept volumes of Balzac in
his desk ; and **so ardent an** admirer was he,
that **having** inherited **a** hundred thousand
francs [1] **from his** mother, he found nothing
better **to do than to** come to Paris to spend
those hundred thousand francs, as they **are**
spent in the pages of Balzac. The project
was put into execution in the most method-
ical manner—bouquets were offered, gloved
finger-tips kissed, duchesses conquered,
courtesans with tawny eyes bought ; nothing
was wanting, the whole crowned by a wild
orgie, modelled upon that in the *Peau de*

---

[1] Four thousand pounds.

Chagrin. The *Peau de Chagrin*, that is to say, the hundred thousand francs, had lasted exactly six months. The son of the great Hellenist had amused himself prodigiously. With his pocket empty and his head full of rhymes, he declared he would henceforth only follow the calling of a poet! But fate decreed that, till the day of his death, Philoxène should be the victim of the author of his fancy. Throwing aside Balzac, he chanced upon Shakespeare. Balzac had only devoured his money, Shakespeare devoured his life. One morning, perhaps it was the consequence of a dream, Philoxène awoke head over ears in love with the works of Shakespeare. And as this man, at once weak and determined, gentle and violent, could do nothing by halves, from that morning, henceforward, he devoted himself body and soul to Shakespeare! To study Shakespeare, to know him by heart, from his most obscure sonnet to his most contested play, was nothing, and that part of the business only took a few months. But Philoxène had the pretension to do better than that : wishing to write a book upon

Shakespeare, a book that should be complete, final, in a word, worthy of the divinity;
he conceived the impracticable project of
reading first everything, absolutely everything, without omitting the least little article
or most insignificant document that has been
published upon Shakespeare for the last two
hundred years up to the present day, in order
to extract from it all
its innermost essence.
Then began a piling up
of dusty folios enough
to build the tower of
Babel :   and,   alas !
Babel it was very soon
in the head of the un-
fortunate Philoxène.

I have seen him at home, no longer master
in his own house, but overpowered on all
sides by Shakespeare. Five thousand, nay,
perhaps ten thousand volumes on Shakespeare, of all shapes, in all languages,
reaching up to the ceiling, obstructing the
windows, invading the armchairs, loading
the tables, heaped up, falling down, choking
both air and light, and in the midst of it all

was Philoxène, taking notes while his brats
wrangled around him. For he was married,
he did not quite know why or
how; and even in some moment
of abstraction between two
studies, had
    had
children.
Over excit-
ed by his
one idea,
    talking
aloud to
himself with
a vacant
gaze, lost in
his dreams,
he wander-
ed through Paris like a blind
man. His wife, a gentle,
saddened creature, followed
him everywhere and acted as
his Antigone. It was she who
mixed his absinthe with the
utmost care; a mild absinthe
scarcely tinted with the green opal coloured

liquid, for the poetic enthusiast had no need of
stimulants. She was to be seen also, seated in
the front row at the conferences held by Philoxène, always upon Shakespeare, in the hall on
the Quay Malaquais. Sometimes the right
word would not come. Painful spectacle ! in
vain the orator sought for it, in vain he knit his
brow ; every one felt that in that encumbered
brain, ideas and phrases jostled each other,
unable to make their escape, like a frightened
crowd struggling at a door in a fire. The
wife, guessing the missing word, would softly
and maternally prompt it. The phrase was
started, flew forth, and then in the midst of
this painful improvisation, of this frenzied
gesticulation, there would be flashes of
brilliance, and brief bursts of eloquence.
There was a true poet within this gentle
lunatic. Philoxène ended sadly, working at
obscure writings to earn a bare pittance and the
wherewithal to buy books, always dreaming
of his great study without being able to write
it. For he would fain read everything written
upon Shakespeare ; and every day there
appeared in Germany or England works
which distanced him, obliging him to put

off once more till some other day the com-
mencement of his own book. He died,
leaving as the only outcome of his life's
work, two short acts written in collaboration
with Théodore de Banville, an unfinished
Polichinelle, sufficiently original in fancy, and
since then reshaped by the makers of such
things; and a volume of verses, gathered
together and published by the tender care
of his friends. A situation as post-mistress
was obtained for his widow, who, after long
mourning her poet, married again some two
years ago, you will never guess whom—
the postman.

Was I not right to draw your attention to
Philoxène and his wife? For myself, I can
never forgot them, and I see them still, shy and
timid, in a corner of the little drawing-room :
he, agitated by spasms of nervousness, she,
holding her breath with astonishment, while
Pagans, just returned from the country of
the orange and the lemon, sang Spanish
songs, and Madame de Chodsko poured out
a pale and vapid decoction called tea—real
exile's tea—for the handsome Polish women
whose heavy bright russet locks lay twisted

in great masses at the back of the head.
As midnight struck the excellent M. Chodsko
appeared with the regularity of a cuckoo in a
clock, bed candle in hand, at the door, cast
over the company a comprehensive glance,

mumbled with a strong Slav accent : "Good
evening, gentlemen," to people who were
never even introduced to him and whom he
never knew, and then disappeared mechanically among the folds of a portière.

The longing to show off my coat led me
sometimes further afield,—right away,—to
the other end of Paris, on the opposite side of
the Seine. To get there, one followed the
quays for some distance, greeted by the odour
of wild beasts, and the roaring of the lions

from behind
the railing of
the Jardin des Plantes ;
then over a bridge, from
which one contemplated by the gaslight or the
moonlight, the fantastic frontage and quaintly
pierced spire of the ruins of the Hôtel
Lavalette ; next came the Arsenal, the old
Arsenal, now a library, with its long iron railings, its great flight of steps, its doorway of

the time of Vauban, decorated with sculptured representations of old-fashioned cannon, and rich, to this day, in recollections of Charles Nodier. Nodier, was no longer there, the famous little green drawing-room where romanticism had its beginning, where Musset, Hugo and Georges Sand shed tears over the adventures of Brisquet's dog—the little green drawing-room more celebrated, and justly so, than the blue drawing-room of Arthénice, was at this time occupied by M. Eugène Loudun.

The spirit of revolution and liberty of thought floated no longer among the curtains. After the champions of romance, had come workmen poets, Christian versifiers, stealing into this eighth palace of the King of Bohemia. Of the old romantic school, only one remained, faithful and unfaltering at his post, stiff and upright in his frock-coat, like an old Huguenot soldier in his armour.

This was Amédée Pommier, a wonderful manufacturer of words and rhymes, the friend of the Dondeys and the Pétrus Borels, the author of *L'Enfer*, of *Crâneries et Dettes de Cœur*—fine books with flaring titles, delight of the literary, horror of the academies, and full of verses, noisy and gaudy as a flight of tropical birds.

Amédée Pommier was a poor and worthy fellow. He led a secluded life, gaining his daily bread by making, for the firm of Hachette, translations which he did not even sign. One curious detail must not be overlooked : it was in collaboration with Amédée Pommier that Balzac, always tormented by the desire to write a great classic comedy, had undertaken *Orgon*, five acts in verse, as a sequel to *Tartufe.*

It was also in the green drawing-room of the Arsenal that I became acquainted with M. Henri de Bornier. He often recited wittily turned little poems, one amongst others I particularly remember, of which each verse ended with this refrain : " Ah! ah! I am not such a fool!" Not such a fool indeed was M. Bornier! for it is he who has written *La Fille de Roland*, which met with so much success at the Théâtre Français and which should some day bring its author to a chair in the Academy. On certain evenings there was a great commotion ;

screens were arranged, chairs and armchairs
arrayed in line, and charades acted. I
even, I must confess, have figured in these
charades, and I can still see myself dressed
as a Circassian slave, shrouded in long,
flowing white veil, in the middle of a
Turkish market. Madame Bornier was my
companion in slavery, while M. Bornier in
turban and caftan, represented some kind of
sultan who purchased us. As for the slave
dealer who sold us, it was, saving your
presence, no less a person than M. L——,
senator, quondam minister, much before the
public at that time and convicted since of
financial irregularities. The fall of the
Empire held many surprises in store for
us; and the great highways of Paris have
sometimes strange windings.

MY DRUMMER.

I WAS at home, and still in bed, one morning, when there was a knock at the door.

" Who's there ? "

" A man with a large case ! "

I naturally fancied that some parcel had arrived from the railway, but instead of the looked-for railway porter, a little man with the round hat and the short jacket of the Provençal shepherd greeted my eyes in the yellow light of the November day. I beheld two black eyes, anxious and gentle, an obstinate, and at the same time, ingenuous face, half lost behind thick moustaches, an accent

flavoured **with garlic,** savouring outrageously
of the sunny south.   The man said,

"I am **Buisson,"** and held out an envelope,
on which I immediately recognized the pretty
and regular handwriting of the poet, Frédéric
Mistral.   **His** letter was brief.   "I send you
friend Buisson; he is a performer **on the**
drum, and wishes **to** make himself known in
Paris.   Pilot **him."**

Pilot a drummer!   **These** southerners have
no conscience!

Having read the letter, I turned to Buisson.

"So **you** are a drummer?"

"Yes, M. Daudet, and the best of them
all; you shall see!"

He went to fetch his instruments, which
he had discreetly left on the landing, behind
the door: a small, long, flat box, and a large
cylinder covered **with** green baize, the same
shape and **size as** the immense *tourniquets*
that the sellers of **sweet** wafers drag about
the streets.   **The** small flat box contained
the *galoubet,* **the** simple rustic flute or fife,
which says "**tu—tu," while** the drum growls
"**pan—pan."   The** covered cylinder was the
tabor (or drum) itself.   What a drum it was!

Tears came into my eyes when I saw it
unwrapped : a real authentic tabor of Louis
XIV.'s time, touching and comical at the
same time in its hugeness, and growling like
an old man if only the tip of a finger touched
it. It was made of fine walnut wood, orna-
mented with light carvings, polished, slight,
light, sonorous, and mellowed as it were by
the touch of time. Solemn as a judge,
Buisson hung his tabor over his left arm,
took up the flute between three fingers of his
left hand, (you have seen the attitude and the
instrument in some antiquated engravings of
the eighteenth century, or painted on a plate
of old *Moustier,*) and handling with the right
hand the little stick tipped with ivory, he
attacked the large drum, which, with its
sonorous vibrations, and its sharp whirr like
that of a grasshopper, marked the rhythm,
and formed a deep bass accompaniment to
the sharp and shrill warbling of the flute.
"Tu—tu—pan—pan! Lo! Paris was far
off, and so was winter. I was transported to
Provence, to the shores of a blue sea, under
the shade of the poplars of the Rhone ;
serenades of the night and of the dawn

resounded beneath the windows. I heard
the singing of carols, saw the country dances
of the *Olivettes*, of the *farandole* winding
beneath the leafy plane-trees of the village
greens, along the dusty whiteness of the high
roads, amongst the lavender of the sunburnt
hill sides; disappearing, reappearing, more
and more impassioned and fantastic, while
the drummer followed slowly, with even

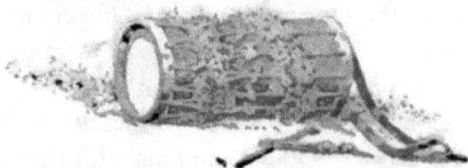

step, sure that the dance would not forsake
the music by the way; solemn, grave, and
hobbling a little, with the movement of the
knee, which at every step pushes the drum
on in front of him.

So many things in the beat of a drum!

Yes! and many more, that you, perhaps,
could not have seen, but which to me were
vividly present. Such is the Provençal imagination: made of tinder, and inflammable,

even at seven o'clock in the morning; and
Mistral did right in counting upon my
enthusiasm.

Buisson also became excited. He told

me of his struggles, his efforts, and how,
midway on the downward path, he had
saved fife and drum from desecration.

Some barbarians, it appeared, wished to

improve the fife by adding two holes to it—
a fife with five holes! what a sacrilege! He
held religiously to the fife with three holes—
the fife of his ancestors, without nevertheless
fearing any rival in the suavity of his slurs,
or the vivacity of his variations and shakes.

"It occurred to me," said he with a
modest air of vague inspiration, and with
that particular accent of the south which
renders comical, even the most touching of
funeral orations. "It occurred to me at
night, one time when I was sitting under an
olive tree, and listening to the nightingale;
and I thought to myself: What! Buisson!
can a wild bird of the good God's sing like
that, and what it can do with one hole, art
thou not man enough to manage with three?"
Somewhat stupid in its pomposity, no doubt,
this platitude, but that morning it struck me
as charming.

A good southerner cannot thoroughly enjoy an emotion unless he can share it with
others. I admired Buisson: others must
admire him also. Behold me then, rushing
all over Paris, showing off my drummer, pre-
senting him everywhere as a phenomenon;

hunting up friends, organizing a *soirée* at my own house. Buisson played and related his struggles, and again said, "It occurred to me." He was decidedly fond of that phrase, and my friends were kind enough, on hearing him, to appear marvellously struck by his talent.

But this was only the first step. At that time a play of mine, a Provençal play, was being rehearsed at the Ambigu. I recommended Buisson, his drum and his fife, to Hostein, the *impresario*, and you may fancy with what eloquence! During eight days, I ceaselessly extolled him. At last Hostein said,

"Suppose we put your drummer into the play? It wants a peg to catch the fancy of the public."

I am sure the Provençal lost his sleep from excitement. The next day, we all three got into a cab; he, the drum, and myself, and, at twelve for the quarter past, as the notices of rehearsal say, we were deposited amid a crowd of idlers, gathered together by the strange appearance of the machine, in front of that low, shamefaced little door-way, which in even the most luxurious theatres, serves as the unostentatious entrance alike for authors, actors, and underlings of all kinds.

"Good Heavens, how dark it is!" sighed the Provençal, as we followed the long passage; —damp and windy as all theatre passages— "how dark it is, and how cold!"

The drum seemed of the same opinion, knocking itself against all the windings of the passages, the steps of the corkscrew staircase, with many vibrations and much formidable rumbling. At last, limping and hobbling, we reached the stage. The rehearsal had begun. Thus seen, in all the barrenness of its undress, a theatre presents a most disenchanting appearance; devoid of movement and life, without the tinsel and brightness of the evening, full of busy folk stepping softly, and their low-voiced talk sounding as far off as if it came from shades on the banks of the Styx, or miners at the bottom of a mine. A smell of mouldy damp, and of escaping gas pervaded everything. Men and things, the moving crowd, all were fantastically mixed up with the scenery, and all wore the same dust-coloured hue, in the mean and paltry light of small hanging lamps,

and gas jets protected with wire gauze, like Davy lamps. And, as if to make the darkness more heavy, the subterranean sensation

more forcible, from time to time, far aloft,
on the second or third tier of the darkened
house, the door of a box would open, and,
as if from the far away mouth of a well, let
fall a ray of external light. This sight, new
to my countryman, slightly unnerved him.
But my fine fellow soon recovered himself,
and pluckily took his place, alone in the
shadow at the back of the stage, on a
barrel that had been got ready for him.
With his drum, it had the effect of two
barrels, one on the top of another. In vain
did I protest : in vain did I say : "In Provence the drummers play as they walk, and
your barrel is impossible." Hostein assured
me that my drummer was a strolling minstrel,
and that a minstrel could only be represented
on the stage on a barrel. Very well ! then
have the barrel ! Moreover, Buisson, full of
self-reliance, had already clambered up, and
was stamping about to find a steady balance,
saying to me : "It does not matter !" We
left him therefore, his fife at his lips, his
drum-stick in his hand, behind a dense forest
of scenery, side pieces, pulleys and ropes ;
and we all, director, author, and actors,

settled ourselves in the front of the stage, as far off as possible, the better to judge the effect.

"It occurred to **me—**" sighed Buisson from out of the darkness, "it occurred **to me** at night, one time when I **was sitting under** an olive tree, listening **to the nightingale—**"

"That will do, that will **do; play us** something!" **I cried out, already exasperated** by his phrase.

Tu—tu—! Pan—Pan—!

"Hush! he is beginning."

"We shall be able to judge of the effect!"

Great heavens! what an effect was produced upon this sceptical audience, by this rustic music, bleating and shrill as the noise of an insect, buzzing over there in a corner! I saw the jeering actors, **always** professionally delighting in the failure of a comrade, ironically pucker up their smooth lips: the fireman under his gas jet, was laughing fit to split his sides; the prompter himself, drawn out **of** his usually somnolescent state by the **strange-** ness of the occurrence, raised himself up on both hands, and peered out of his box, looking like a gigantic tortoise. However, Buisson having finished playing, again began his

phrase, which he apparently thought very
telling :

"What! can a wild bird of the good
God's sing like that, and what it can do with
one hole, art thou not man enough to manage
with three !"

"What is this fellow of yours talking about,
with his story of holes?" asked Hostein.

Then I tried to explain **the** point of the
matter, the importance of the three holes
instead of five ; the originality there was in
playing alone, the two instruments. "The
fact is," observed Marie Laurent, "it would
be infinitely more convenient if they were
played by two persons."

I tried, in order to strengthen my argument,
to sketch out a *farandole* step on the stage.
It was of no avail, **I** began vaguely to understand the sad truth, that, to make others feel
the impressions and poetical recollections
evoked in my bosom by the drummer and
his old-fashioned airs, the musician should
have been able to bring at the same time to
Paris, the top of a hill side, a space of blue
sky, **a** whiff of the warm Provençal atmosphere : "Come, my children, get on, get on !

And without bestowing any further notice on the drummer, the rehearsal continued. Buisson never stirred, and remained at his post, feeling certain of success, and honestly believing that he was already acting a part in the play. After the first act, a feeling of remorse came over me, at leaving him over there on his barrel, where only his outline could vaguely be seen.

"Come, Buisson, get down, quick."

"Are we going to begin?"

The unfortunate fellow thought he had made a wonderful effect, and showed me a stamped paper, an agreement already prepared with the foresight characteristic of the peasant.

"No, not to-day; they will write to you; but take care! hang it! your drum knocks against everything, and makes a frightful row." I felt now quite ashamed of the drum, I trembled lest any one should hear it, and oh! what a joy and relief it was, when I got it back into the cab! For a week I did not venture to return to the theatre.

Shortly afterwards, Buisson came again to see me.

" Well ! how about that agreement ? "

" That agreement ? **Ah yes!** that agreement. Well, **Hostein hesitates ;** he does not understand."

" He's a fool ! "

On hearing the bitter and harsh tone in which the gentle musician pronounced these words, I realized the extent of my crime. Intoxicated by my enthusiasm, and my praise ; his equilibrium upset, and losing all sense of proportion, the Provençal drummer seriously believed himself a great genius, and expected—alas ! had I not led him to expect it—that Paris held in store for him endless triumphs.

How could one stop a drum, uproariously careering through the rocks and thorny thickets of the slopes of imagination !

I did not even attempt it : it would have been madness, and labour lost.

Moreover, Buisson had now found some other admirers, and amongst the greatest celebrities,—Felicien David, and Théophile Gautier, to whom Mistral had written at the same time as to me. Poetic and dreamy spirits, easily charmed, prone to abstraction, the author of a *Journey in the East*, and the musician of the land of roses, had found no trouble in creating in their minds' eye a landscape around the rustic melodies of the drummer.

The one fancied, while the fife piped away, that he saw once more the shores of his native Durance, and the half ruined terraces on the slopes of Cadenet : while the dreams of the other carried him still further away, and he found in the dull and monotonous sound of the drum I know not what charming memories of nights at the Golden Horn and of Arab *derboukas*.

Both had been smitten with a sudden and violent caprice for Buisson's real talent, here however so out of harmony with all its surroundings.

For a whole fortnight there were incessant puffs in the newspapers about the drummer ; the illustrated papers were full of his portraits, in an attitude of proud defiance, and a conquering look, the light flute between his fingers, the drum slung over his shoulder. Intoxicated with his success, Buisson bought the papers by the dozen, and despatched them to his own country.

From time to time, he came to see me and
to relate his triumphs : smoking parties made
up for him in some artists' studios, a few
evenings spent in fashionable society in the
Faubourg Saint Germain (he was full of the
Faubourg de Séïnt Germéïn, as he called it),
where the fellow brought back tender dreams
to the old turbaned
dowagers, as he re-
peated without the
slightest bashfulness
his famous phrase : " It
occurred to me at
night, one time, when
I was sitting under
an olive tree and
listening to the night-
ingale." Meanwhile,
as he was afraid of getting rusty, and
wished, in spite of the thousand amusements
of an artist's life, to keep up the mellowness
of his touch and the delicacy of his mouth-
piece, our ingenious Provençal conceived the
idea of rehearsing his serenades and his
farandoles, in the very heart of Paris, on
the fifth floor of the furnished lodgings he

was occupying in the Quartier Breda. Tu—
tu! Pan—pan! The whole Quartier protested wrathfully against this unwarrantable
disturbance. The neighbours gathered together and made a formal complaint; but

Buisson only continued the more, spreading
around him a wide circle of harmony and
sleeplessness; till one evening the door
porter, utterly worn out, refused him the
key of his room.

Draping himself in all the dignity of an

artist, Buisson appealed to the magistrates,
and gained his cause. French laws, so hard
on musicians, relegating the performance on
the horn to the depths of the cellars all the
year round, with the exception of Shrove
Tuesday, allowing them only one day out
of three hundred and sixty-five on which to
flourish their brass instruments in the open
air; the French law it appears, had not
foreseen the Provençal drum.

After this victory Buisson no longer
doubted his own powers. One Sunday
morning I received a card: that afternoon
he was going to make his appearance at a
large concert in the Salle du Châtelet. Duty
and friendship compelled my attendance, I
therefore went to hear him, not without a
secret misgiving, and sad forebodings.

A capital house, full from the pit to the
roof; decidedly our puffs and notices had
borne fruit. Suddenly, amid the general
excitement and breathless silence, the curtain drew up. I uttered a cry of amazement.
Alone, in the centre of the stage, on which
six hundred supernumeraries can be man-
œuvred without crowding, stood Buisson and

his drum, dressed up in a skimpy coat and wearing a pair of gloves which made him look like those long, yellow-legged insects that Granville (the famous caricaturist) portrays in his whimsical drawings, furiously playing on the most fantastical instruments. Buisson alone stood before us. I could see him through the opera glass, waving his long arms, fluttering his elytra; evidently the unhappy fellow was playing, drumming with all his might, blowing with all his strength; but not the faintest note reached the audience. It was too far off, all the sound was swallowed up by the stage. It was like a baker's cricket chirping his serenade in the middle of the Champ de Mars! Impossible to count the flute holes at this distance, impossible to repeat the phrase: "It occurred to me," or to mention the "bird of the good God's!"

I blushed with mortification. Around me I saw nothing but amazement, and I heard the muttered words, "What poor joke is this?" The doors of the boxes slammed, the house, little by little, was emptying; however as it was a polite audience, they did not hiss him, but quietly left the drummer to end his tune in solitude.

I waited for him at the door to console him. Well! would you believe it! He fancied he had had an immense success, and more radiant than ever, exclaimed, "I am waiting for Colonne to sign!" at the same time showing me a large paper covered with official stamps. This time it was more than I could bear, I plucked up my courage and said roughly, all in a breath, what I thought.

"Buisson, we have all been mistaken in trying to make Paris understand the charm of your large drum; the melody of your fife. I have made a mistake, Gautier and David have made a mistake, and, as a natural consequence, you also have made a mistake. No, you are not the nightingale."

"It occurred to me," interrupted Buisson.

"Yes, I know it occurred to you, but you are not a nightingale. The nightingale sings everywhere, his songs are the songs of every country, and in every country his songs are understood. You are only a poor little cicala, whose monotonous and dry note is in harmony with the pale olive trees, the pines weeping their rosin in tears of gold, the brilliant blue sky, the glorious sun, the stony hill-sides of Provence ; but here, under this gray sky, midst rain and wind, you are nothing but a ridiculous, lamentable grasshopper with long damp wings. Return home, take back your drum, sing your love songs by daybreak and by twilight, play to the girls while they dance their *farandoles,* lead the triumphal march of the conquerors in the bull fights; down there you are a poet, an artist ; here you are nothing but a misunderstood mountebank."

He did not answer, but in his mystic glance, in his gently obstinate eye, I read his thought : "My friend, you are jealous of me !"

A few days later, my fine fellow, proud as "Artaban," came to tell me that Colonne—another fool, like Hostein !—had refused to sign, but that another affair was offered to him, marvellous this time, an engagement in a *café* concert at a hundred and twenty francs a night, all settled and signed beforehand. He showed me the paper. Ah ! what a capital paper ! I learnt the truth later on.

I know not what puzzled director, borne away and blinded by the muddy current of bankruptcy, desperately seized upon that broken reed—Buisson's pitiful music. Certain that he would never pay, he signed all that was asked. But the Provençal did not see so far ahead ; he had it down on stamped paper, and this stamped paper was sufficient for his happiness. Moreover, as it was a music hall, a costume was necessary.

"They have dressed me up as a Troubadour of the olden time," he said with a gracious smile, "but as I am very well made, it suits me, you will see." I did see !

It was one of those music halls near the Porte Saint Denis, so much in vogue during the last years of the Empire ; with the tinsel of the barbarous ornamentation, half Chinese, half Persian ; its daubs and gilding rendered more glaring by the exaggerated number of gas jets and lustres, and with closed and latticed boxes, in which, on certain evenings, duchesses and ambassadresses hid themselves to applaud the strange contortions or vulgar songs of some eccentric diva. A sea of heads and beer glasses all levelled like waves in foggy weather by the dense smoke of the pipes and the vapour of breath ; the waiters running about, the consumers shouting their orders ; and all

dominated by the orchestra leader, white-
tied, impassible and dignified, raising or
calming with the gesture of a Neptune, the
tempest of fifty brass instruments. Between
the ridiculously sentimental song, bleated out
by a somewhat pretty girl, with sheepish
eyes; and an eclogue as hot as cayenne
pepper, cynically bawled by a kind of
Thérèsa with red arms, there appeared on
the stage, in front of a semi-circle of some
six simpering and yawning women in low
white dresses, a personage whose appearance
in all my life long I shall never forget. It
was Buisson, the fife between his fingers, the
drum on his left knee, in Troubadour costume,
as he had threatened. But what a Troubadour! A jerkin (imagine such a thing!) half
apple-green, half blue; one leg red, the other
yellow, the whole attire so tight fitting that it
made one shudder; a crenelated cap, shoes
turned up like a jester's; and with all this,
moustaches, his magnificent moustaches, too
long and too black, which he could not bring
himself to sacrifice, falling over his chin like
a cascade of blacking!

Carried away apparently by the exquisite

taste of this costume, the public greeted the
musician with a long murmur of applause,
and my Troubadour smirked with pleasure,
and was happy at seeing before him this
sympathetic audience, and feeling at his
back a warm glow of inflammatory glances
from the admiring and lovely creatures seated
in a half-circle behind him. It was quite
another affair however when the music began. The tu-tu, pan-pan, failed to please
the vitiated taste of ears surfeited by the
vitriol-like *repertoire* of the place, as a palate
loses its discrimination by the abuse of
spirits. Then too it was not a distinguished and well-mannered company like that
at the Châtelet. " Enough ! Enough !
Take him away ! Shut up, squeaker ! "
Vainly did Buisson try to open his mouth
and to say : " It occurred to me." The
audience rose, the curtain had to be lowered,
and the red, green, blue and yellow Troubadour, disappeared in a storm of hissing and
hooting, like some poor draggled parrot,
eddying round in a tropical hurricane.

Would you believe it ? Buisson persisted !
An illusion springs up quickly in a Provençal

brain, and is difficult to uproot. Fifteen
evenings running he reappeared, always
hissed, never paid ; till the moment arrived
when the sheriff's officer came to fix a notice of
bankruptcy upon the open iron work of the
concert hall gates.

Then began the downfall of Buisson. From
one low pothouse to another, lower and lower
still, always believing in his success, always
pursuing his chimera of an engagement made
on stamped paper, the drummer trundled at
last to the tea-gardens of the suburbs, where
the players are only paid by the hour, have
no other orchestra than a toothless piano,
and form the delight of a public composed of
tipsy and tired canoeists and counterjumpers
out for their Sunday holiday.

One evening—the winter was scarcely over
and the spring not yet begun—I was crossing
the Champs Elysées. An open air concert,
wishing to get the start of the others, had
already hung its lanterns in the still leafless
trees. There was a slight drizzle, an air of
melancholy over all. Suddenly I heard
Tu—Tu—Pan—Pan !— There he was
again ! I saw him through the opening,

drumming away at a Provençal air, before
some half dozen auditors, favoured no doubt
with orders, and sheltering themselves under
umbrellas.   I dare not go in! "It was my
fault," I thought, "after all! The fault of my
imprudent enthusiasm."   Poor Buisson ! Poor
half-drowned grasshopper !

"TARTARIN DE TARASCON."

THE STORY OF MY BOOKS.

ALTHOUGH it is now nearly fifteen years since I published the *Adventures of Tartarin*, Tarascon has not yet forgiven me for writing them ; and travellers worthy of belief assure me that every morning, when that tiny Provençal town opens the shutters of its shops and shakes its carpets in the balmy breath of the great Rhone, there breaks forth from every threshold and from every window, a united fury of clenched fists and flaming black eyes, one vast cry of rage directed towards Paris. "Oh that Daudet ! If for once he came this way !" As Bluebeard says in the story, " Come down, or I come up."

And without joking, one day, Tarascon did " come up ! "

It was in 1878, when Provincials swarmed in the hotels, on the boulevards, and on that gigantic bridge connecting the Champ de Mars and the Trocadéro. One morning, the sculptor Amy, a native of Tarascon, naturalized in Paris, beheld, piercing their way into his house, a formidable pair of moustaches, arrived by the excursion train, under pretext of seeing the Exhibition, but in reality to have an explanation with Daudet on the subject of the brave Commandant Bravida, and the *Défense de Tarascon*, a little tale published by me during the war.

" *Qué?*—we will go to that Daudet ! "

It was always the first word of those Tarascon moustaches on entering the studio ; and for a whole fortnight, the sculptor Amy had this phrase ringing in his ears : "And now then, where shall we find that Daudet?" The unfortunate artist was at his wits' end to find any way of sparing me this serio-comic visit. He took the moustaches of his

compatriot to the Exhibition, lost them in the
gallery of "dwellings of all nations," in the
machinery department ; poured down their
throat English beer, Hungarian wines, mares'
milk, and every exotic and varied drink he
could find ; deafened them with music of all
kinds : Moorish, Tzigane, Japanese ; worried
them, tired them to death, and dragged them
—like Tartarin on his minaret—to the sum-
mit of the Trocadéro turrets.

But the enmity of the Provençal rankled
deep, and even from this lofty height, spying
over Paris, he said with a frown,

" Can we see his house ? "

" Whose house ? "

" *Tè !*—why Daudet's of course ! "

It was the same thing everywhere.
Happily the excursion train got up steam
again, and carried away the unsatisfied ven-
geance of the Tarascon ; but although that
one had departed, others might arrive, and
all the time the Exhibition was open, I never
slept.

It is a serious affair, after all, to feel
concentrated upon one's self the hatred of a
whole town. Even now, whenever I go

south, I feel an awkwardness in passing
Tarascon; I know they still bear me a
grudge, that my books are prohibited in
their libraries, are not even to be found at
the railway bookstalls; and from the first
moment I behold through the railway carriage
window the castle of good King Réné, I feel
myself ill at ease, and long to whisk past
that station.

This is why I seize the opportunity afforded
me by this new edition, to offer publicly with
my apologies, to the people of Tarascon, the
explanation which the former commander-in-
chief of their militia came at that time to
demand of me.

Tarascon was for me only a pseudonym
picked up on the way from Paris to Marseilles,
because it had a fine sonorous roll in the
accent of the South, and sounded as the
name of the station was shouted, like the
triumphant war-cry of an Apache warrior.
In reality, the home of Tartarin, and the
scene of the famous cap-shooting parties is
a little farther off, five or six leagues on the
other side of the Rhone. There it was that
as a child, I watched the baobab tree, lan-

guishing in the confinement of its tiny
mignonette pot, faithful image of my hero,
cramped within the precincts of his little
town ; there the Rebuffas sang the duet from
Robert le Diable; from thence it was, in short,
that in November, 1861, Tartarin and I,
armed to the teeth and *chechia* on head,
started to hunt the lion in Africa. To tell
the truth, I did not go there altogether ex-
pressly for that purpose, being desirous above
all things, of repairing my somewhat dilapidated lungs in the warm sunshine. But not
in vain, heaven be praised, was I born in the
land of the mighty cap-shooters ! and from
the moment I set foot on the deck of the
Zouave, where they were getting on board
our enormous case of arms, I imagined, more
Tartarin than Tartarin himself, that I was
going to exterminate all the wild beasts of
the Atlas.

Ah, what a fairy tale was that first voyage !
How vividly I can recall the moment of
departure ; the blue sea before me—blue as
cobalt—all ruffled by the wind, flecked with
sparkling spray, and the bowsprit of the
vessel, which again and again rose in the air,

dipped in the wave, trembled a moment all
white with foam, and ever pointed seawards ;
once more I hear in the broad sunlight, the
hour of noon strike from all the clocks of
Marseilles, and once more my twenty years
of life ring in my head a joyous peal.

Merely to speak of it, brings it all before
me again : I am over there, I haunt the
bazaars of Algiers in a semi-daylight which
is scented with musk, amber, dried rose
leaves and warm woollen stuffs. Three-
stringed guzlas are twanging before the little
glass-fronted Tunisian cupboards, arabesqued
in mother-o'-pearl, while the plash of the
fountain throws a fresh note of sound upon
the tiles of the court-yard. I see myself
ranging the Sahel, the orange groves of
Blidah, the Chiffa, the famous brook of
monkeys ; wandering over the green slopes
of Milianah, its orchards tangled with bottle-
gourds, sunflowers and fig-trees, as in the
walled enclosures of our own Provence.

Once more the immense valley of Chélif
lies before me, with its thick brushwood of
lentisk and dwarf palms, and the dry beds of
torrents edged with oleanders ; on the hori-

zon, the smoke of a camp fire rises straight
upwards from a thicket of cactus, nearer, the
gray circle trampled by a caravan, a saint's
tomb with its white turban-like cupola, its
thank-offerings hung on the dazzling, white-
washed wall, and here and there, in the wide,

burnt-up space, a few dark, moving spots
which I know to be cattle.

I hear again, accompanied by the horrible
shaking of my Arab saddle, the clink of my
great stirrups, the cry of the shepherds
rebounding through the still and clear at-

mosphere : " *Si mohame—e—ed—i,*" the furious barking of the *slougi* dogs round the camps, the firing and howling of an Arab *fantasia* and the wild music of *derboukas*, played in the evening before the tent doors, while jackals yelp in the plains, persevering like our grasshoppers, and above all rises in the star-spangled blackness of the night sky, a faint crescent of the moon—the crescent of Mohammed. Very distinct too in my memory is the dreariness of the return ; the feeling of exile and cold on arriving at Marseilles, where the blue of our Provençal sky seemed to me dulled and veiled by comparison with those clear and vast Algerian skies, filled as they were with the most intense and varied range of colour : with the wonderful green of the sunrise—a poisonous, arsenical green ; with the brief twilights of the evening changing and trembling through mother-o'-pearl tints of purple and amethyst ; where the wells were rose-coloured, and rose-coloured camels came to drink, and the chain of the well and the beard of the Bedouin who drank from the same bucket, all glittered with rose-tinted drops ;—after a lapse of

twenty years, I feel again the regret and
longing for the breadth of that African sunshine left behind me.

There is in the language of the poet Mistral,
a word which comprises and defines clearly
a whole instinct of the race : *galéja*, to joke,
to make fun. And it conveys to the mind
the flash of irony, the sparkle of malice,
shining in the depths of the Provençal eyes.
Galéja recurs on all occasions in the conversation, in the form of a verb or substantive.
"*Vessés pàs ? Es uno galéjado.* Don't you
see ? It is only a joke. *Taisoté, galéjaïré.*
Hold your tongue, naughty jester." But to
be *galéjaïré* does not exclude from the
character either kindness or tenderness.
They amuse themselves, *té !* they must laugh ;
but in that country, laughter is the accompaniment of every sentiment, of the
deepest as of the most tender. In an old,
old song of my beloved mother-country, the
history of little Fleurance, this Provençal
love of laughter is exquisitely exemplified.
Fleurance, when almost a child, is betrothed
to a knight, who marries her, *la prén tan
jouveneto se saup pas courdela,* when so young

that she can scarcely tie for herself the lacing
of her bodice.   Scarcely is the honeymoon
over when Fleurance's lord is obliged to
start for Palestine, leaving his little bride all
alone.   Seven years pass by, and the knight
has given no sign of life, when one day, a
pilgrim with cockle
shell and long beard
presents himself at the
gate of the castle.
He has returned from
the wars; he brings
news of the husband
of Fleurance; and at
once the fair lady
causes him to be ad-
mitted and places him
him at table opposite
to her.

What happened be-
tween them then I can relate to you in two
ways; for the story of Fleurance, like all popular
songs, has made the round of France in the
pedlars' packs, and I found it in Picardy with a
significant variation. In the Picardy version the
lady begins to weep in the middle of the feast.

"You weep, fair Fleurance?" says the
pilgrim all trembling.

"I weep because I recognize you—you are
my dear husband."

The little Fleurance of Provence, cn the

contrary, is scarcely seated in front of the
pilgrim with the great beard, before she begins
to laugh delightfully at him, "*Hé!* what are
you laughing at, Fleurance?" "*Té!* I laugh
because you are my husband."

And laughing she jumps upon his knee,

and the pilgrim also laughs in his sham beard of tow ; for he is, as she is, a *galéjaïré ;* all of which does not prevent them from loving each other tenderly, with open arms, with meeting lips, with all the pent emotion of their faithful hearts.

I too am a *galéjaïré.* In the fogs of Paris, in the splashing of her mud, in the sadness lurking in a great city, I may perhaps have lost the taste and faculty of laughter ; but in reading *Tartarin,* any one may see that there then remained in me a store of gaiety which promptly broke forth in the glorious sunlight of " *down there.*"

Certainly, I am willing to admit that many other things might have been written about Algerian France, than the *Adventures of Tartarin ;* for instance, a close and incisive study of manners and customs, the observations of a new country on the confines of two races and two civilizations, with their reflex action ; the conqueror conquered in his turn by the climate, by the profoundly indolent habits, the carelessness, the utter rottenness of the East, the bastinado and thieving, the Algerian Doineau and the Algerian

Bazaine—those two perfect products of the Arab *bureau*. What revelations might be made of the wretchedness of this pioneer existence, this history of a colonist; the foundation of a town in the midst of the rivalry of three presiding powers, army, civil administration, and magistracy. Instead of all that, I brought back nothing but *Tartarin*, a burst of laughter, a *galéjade.* —

It is true that my comrade and I must have appeared a fine pair of simpletons, when we landed in red sashes and gaudy *chechia* in the famous town of Algiers, where we were the only two " *Teurs.*" With what a meditative air of conviction did Tartarin doff his immense hunting boots at the doors of the mosques and gravely penetrate into the sanctuaries of Mohammed, with tight shut lips and in bright coloured socks. Ah! how thoroughly he at least believed in the East, in the muezzins and the almées, in the lions, the panthers, and the dromedaries; in everything that his books had been kind enough to suggest to him, and which his meridional imagination had magnified and exaggerated.

Faithful as the camel of my story, I

followed him through his heroic dream ; but
I had my moments of doubt. I remember
one evening, at Oued-Fodda, starting off to
lie in wait for a lion, how, passing through a
camp **of** *chasseurs* d'*Afrique*, with all our
paraphernalia **of** spatterdashes, guns, re-
volvers and hunting **knives,** I felt a sharp
sensation of ridicule, when I saw the silent
amazement of these worthy troopers cooking
their soup **in** front **of** the long lines of tents.
" And what if after all there is no lion ! "

Nevertheless, an hour later, when night
had fallen, hiding on my knees in a clump of
laurels, sweeping the dark shadows with my
glasses, while the cry of the crane sounded
high up in the sky, and the jackals trampled
the vegetation around me, I felt my gun
chatter and rattle on the handle of the
hunting knife stuck in the ground.

I have invested Tartarin with this shiver
of fear, and the absurd reflections which
accompany it ; but it is doing him a great
injustice. **I can** honestly assure you, that if
the lion had really come, the worthy Tartarin
would have received him rifle in hand, dagger
upraised ; and if his ball had missed, his

sword broken in the huge animal closing
upon him, he would have finished the
struggle hand to hand, would have crushed
the fierce brute in the powerful muscles of
his arms, and torn it to pieces, with his nails
and his teeth, not even stopping to spit out
the fur; for he was a tough fellow at bottom,
this mighty shooter of caps, and moreover a
man of humour who was the first to laugh
at any *galéjade!*

The story of Tartarin was not written till
long after my journey in Algeria. The
journey took place in 1861-62, the book was
written in 1869. I began to publish it in
parts, in the *Petit Moniteur universel*, illustrated with amusing sketches by Emile
Benassit. It was an absolute failure. The
Petit Moniteur was a popular paper, and the
populace are puzzled by printed irony which
makes them think they are being laughed at.
No words can describe the disappointment
of the subscribers to this half-penny paper,
who delighted in *Rocambole* and the writings
of Ponson du Terrail; when they read in the
first chapters of the life of Tartarin, of the
songs, of the baobab tree; their disappoint-

ment even expressed itself in personal abuse
and threats of discontinued subscriptions.
I used to receive letters which said : " Well
then, what follows ? What does all this prove ?
Idiot ! " and then came a furious signature.
Paul Dalloz suffered the most, for he had
gone to great expense in advertisements, and
illustrations, and paid dear for this experience.
After a dozen or so of numbers had appeared,
I took pity on him and carried *Tartarin* to
the *Figaro*, whose readers were better fitted
to understand it, but here it was met by other
conflicting powers. The working editor of
the *Figaro* just then, was Alexandre
Duvernois, brother of Clément Duvernois
quondam journalist and minister. By the
merest chance I had, nine years before, in
the course of my delightful expedition, met
Alexandre Duvernois—at that time a humble
clerk in the civil administration of Milianah,
and who from that date retained a perfect
enthusiasm for the whole Colony. Irritated
and indignant at the frivolous spirit in which
I wrote about his beloved Algeria, he arranged,
although he could not prevent the publication
of *Tartarin*, to cut it up into intermittent

scraps, on the horrible stereotyped pretext of
"press of matter," to such effect, that the
poor little tale dragged its weary length in
the paper, almost as interminably as the
Wandering Jew or the *Three Musketeers.*
"It drags, it drags," grumbled the deep bass
of Villemessant, and I was greatly afraid I
should be obliged to break off once more.

Then came fresh tribulations. The hero of
my book was then called Barbarin of Tarascon.

Now, there unfortunately happened to live
at Tarascon an old family of the name of
Barbarin, who threatened to go to law with
me if I did not at once take their name out
of this outrageous piece of tomfoolery. Having a holy horror of courts of law, and justice
generally, I agreed to replace Barbarin by
Tartarin on the already corrected proofs,
which had therefore to be re-read line by
line in a most scrupulous hunt for the letter
B. In those three hundred pages, a few
managed to escape my notice, and you
may find in the first edition, Bartarin,
Tarbarin, and even *tonsoir* for *bonsoir.* At
last the book was published, and succeeded
well enough in the circulating library, not-

withstanding the local flavour, which could not be to the taste of every one. One must be of the south, or know it very well indeed, to understand how frequent a type amongst us this Tartarin **is, and** how, under the glorious sunshine of Tarascon, which fills its people with warmth and electricity, the wild absurdity of brains and imagination, becomes developed in profoundly exaggerated forms, as varied in shape and dimensions as the fruit of the bottle-gourd.

Judged impartially, at a distance of years, *Tartarin*, with its careless and madcap style, seems to me to possess the qualities of youth, life and truth ; a truth however of beyond the Loire, which exaggerates, dilates, but does **not** lie, and is Tarascon to the backbone all the time. The quality of the writing is neither very finished nor very concise. It is what I venture to call "peripatetic literature," spoken, **gesticulated ;** accompanied by all the easy manners of my hero. But I must own, that with all my love of style, of fine prose, harmonious and full of life and colour, that this is not all that is needed, in my opinion, **by** the novelist. His truest joy must always

be to create beings, to set on foot by their
truth to nature types of humanity which
shall thenceforward be known in the world
by the name, the expression and gesture, he
has bestowed upon them, and which have
caused them to be talked of, detested, or
liked, by those who read of them, without
reference to their creator, or without so
much as mentioning his name. For my own
part, my emotion is always the same, when,
à propos of some passer-by, one of the thousand marionnettes of our human comedy,
political, artistic, or of the world, I
hear it said, "He is a Tartarin—a Mon-
pavon—a Delobelle." A thrill runs through
me then, the proud thrill of a father, hidden
amongst the crowd who applaud his son, and
who, all the time is longing to exclaim,
"That is my boy!"

G

THE STORY OF MY BOOKS.

On the road between Arles and the quarries of Fontvielle, after passing the Mont de Corde and the abbey of Montmajour, there rises, on the right-hand side, behind a large village, white with dust as a stone-cutter's yard, a small hillock covered with pine trees; a refreshing patch of green in the midst of the parched landscape. Up above, turned the long arms of a windmill; and below, nestling under the hillside was a

large white house called Montauban, **an old**
building of great originality, **for,** beginning
like **a great country** house, with a **flight of**
steps **and an Italian terrace supported by**
columns, it finished with **the walls of a *mas***
or country farm, with perches **for the pea-**
cocks, a vine **over the doorway, a well with**
a fig tree twisting round **the iron work, sheds**
under which lie harrows and ploughs, **a**
sheep-pen in front of an **orchard** of slender
almond trees, their **branches of** delicate pink
flowers continually scattered **by the** March
winds. These **are the only flowers of**
Montauban. There are no **lawns, no flower**
beds, no gardens, no enclosures; nothing
but clumps of pine **trees starting from**
amongst the gray rocks, a natural **and wild**
park, full of tangled **pathways, all slippery**
with the dry and fallen **pine needles. Inside**
the **building existed the same** incongruous
mixture of mansion and farm; there were
long galleries, flagged **and cool, furnished**
with cane-twisted sofas **and** armchairs of
the time of **Louis XVI., so** well suited for a
summer siesta : **spacious** stairs, imposing
corridors, **where the wind dashes in, and**

whistling under the doors of the rooms
shakes the old-fashioned striped hangings.
Then, on going up a couple of steps, a
sudden transformation greets the eye ; here
is the large rustic kitchen of the farm, with
its uneven floor of beaten earth, where the
hens scratch to pick up the crumbs of the
farm breakfast, and its whitewashed walls
supporting the walnut-wood shelves and the
quaintly carved bread box and kneading
trough.

Twenty years ago, an old Provençal
family lived there, no less original and
delightful than their dwelling. The mother,
a superior woman of the better class of
farmer, old, but still upright, and wearing the
widow's cap she would never discard,
managed entirely the extensive property,
consisting of olive trees, wheat, vines and
mulberry trees ; near her, were her four
sons, four old bachelors known by the names
of the professions they had practised or were
still exercising : the Mayor, the Consul, the
Notary, the Lawyer. When their father died,
and their sister married, they gathered all
four closely round the old woman, sacrificing

for her sake, their ambitions and their tastes ;
united in an all-powerful bond of love for her
whom they spoke of as "dear Mamma," with
a respectful and tender accent.

Excellent folks ! fortunate household !
How often have I come there in the winter
months to put myself again in touch with
nature, to shake off
Paris and its fevered
life, by the health-giv-
ing scents of our little
Provençal hills.   I
arrived without any
warning, certain of my
welcome, heralded by
the screams of the
peacocks and the
barking of the dogs.
Miracle, *Miraclet*, *Tambour*, jumping up
round the dog-cart, while the Arlesian cap
of the servant girl fluttered with surprise as
she rushed off to inform her masters ; and the
"dear Mamma " pressed me to her little gray
checked shawl as if I had been one of her
own boys.   After five tumultuous minutes,
when the huggings were over, and my trunk

was in my room, the house became again
silent and calm.   As for me I whistled to
old Miracle—a spaniel picked up at sea on
a piece of wreckage by the fishermen of
Faraman—and went up to my windmill.

The windmill was a
ruin, a mass of crumbling
stone, iron, and rotten
wood, which had not been
set to the wind for many
a year, and which lay all
broken and out of gear,
useless as a poet, while all
around on the hill-side,
the busy trade of the
miller prospered, and
sails went merrily round.
What strange affinities lie
within us !   From the
very first this aban-
doned mill was dear to
me, I liked it for its forsaken air, its path
overgrown with grass, the short mountain
grasses, gray and perfumed, full of the little
herbs with which Father Gaucher composes
his elixir; its broken platform, where one

might idly lie, sheltered from the wind, while a rabbit dashed past, or a long adder with creeping and sneaking motion came forth to hunt the field mice with which the ruins were swarming. With the gusts of the *tramontana* shaking the old building till it crackled again, whistling through its shattered sails as if through rigging, the wind-mill awoke in my uneasy and wandering brain memories of past sea voyages, of visits to lighthouses, and distant isles, and the quivering swell all round me completed the illusion. I know not whence I inherit this love of solitude and wild nature, but I have had it from childhood; it seemed so little in harmony with the exuberance of my spirits— unless it can be at the same time a physical necessity for me to repair by a fast of words, an abstinence from talk and gesticulation, the frightful expenditure of his whole being which is a Southerner's life. In any case, I owe much to these mental rests; and no place was ever more healthful to me than this old Provençal windmill. I even thought once of buying it; there might be found yet, among the papers of the notary of Fontvielle,

an agreement of sale, which remained only a
project, but of which I made use, as the
preamble of my book.

My windmill never belonged to me.   But
this did not prevent me from spending there
long days filled with dreams and recollections,
till the sun sank among the little flattened
hills, of which it filled the hollows as with
molten metal, a casting of fiery and glowing
gold. Then, at the sound of a conch-shell,
the horn with which M. Séguin summoned
home his goat, I returned for the evening
repast, at the hospitable and fantastic table of
Montauban, laid according to the tastes and
habits of each member of the party : the
Constantia drunk by the Consul, side by side
with the water gruel, or the plate of boiled
chestnuts which formed the frugal dinner of
the old mother. The coffee drunk, pipes
lighted and the four sons gone off to the village, I remained alone talking with the excellent woman—a good energetic character with
a subtle intelligence and a memory full of
stories, which she related with much simple
eloquence : tales of her childhood, of the departed, of disused customs, the gathering of

the gall nuts on the oak trees of the parish ; of 1815, the invasion, the cry of relief that rose from all mothers' hearts at the fall of the first Empire; the dances, the bonfires lighted in all the market places, and the smart Cossack officer who made her skip like a kid, as they danced all night long on the bridge of Beaucaire. Then came her marriage, the death of her husband ; that of her eldest daughter, which a sad presentiment and a sudden shock of terror revealed to her at a distance of many miles away — mournings, births, and the removal of the cherished remains of her dear ones, when the old cemetery was closed. It was like turning over the leaves of one of those ancient family chronicles, with well worn edges, wherein formerly it was the custom to write down the inner life of the family, mixed with the common details of every-day life, and where the accounts of good years of wine and oil stand

side by side with perfect marvels of self-sacri-
fice and pious resignation.   In this half-rustic
bourgeoise there was I felt, a beautiful soul,
charmingly feminine, delicate, intuitive, allied
to the graceful and ignorant malice of a little
child.   Weary of talking, she would sink back
in her large armchair, far from the lamp,
while the growing
shadows of the
falling night closed
her sunken eye-
lids, slowly crept
over her aged face,
with its long lines
of wrinkles, fur-
rowed as with the
plough and the
harrow; and silent
and motionless, I
might have thought her asleep, had it not
been for the clink of the beads, that
her fingers were telling at the bottom
of her pocket.   Then I softly rose, and
went to end my evening in the large
kitchen.

In the ingle-nook of the gigantic chimney,

where the copper lamp hung, a **numerous company was seated in front of** a bright fire of olive roots, the fitful flame of which fantastically lit up the pointed **caps of** the women and the yellow woollen jackets **of the men.** In the place of honour, **on the hearth-stone,** squatted **the shepherd, with his shaven chin,** tanned skin and his *cachimbau* (short pipe) **stuck in** the **corner of** his well-cut mouth ; **he hardly** spoke, being accustomed **to the** contemplative silence of **his long months of** lonely watching, **far away from** all human companionship, **on the Alps of** Dauphiny, gazing **up at the stars he knew so well,** from *Jen de Milan* down **to the** *Char des âmes.* Between **the** puffs of his pipe, he gave **out in** his sonorous **dialect, sentences, half uttered** parables, and **incomprehensible proverbs,** some of which **I still remember.**

" *The song of Paris, the saddest history in the world. Man in speech and beast by his horns. Monkey's work, little and bad. As the moon wanes, water falls. Red moon, wind changes. White moon, fine day."* And every evening he brought the proceedings **to a close with the** following **sentence.** " *The longer the old woman lived, the more she*

*knew and for that, the less willing was she
to die."*

By his side, the keeper Mitifio, nicknamed
Pistol, with merry twinkling eye, and white,
pointed beard, amused the company, with a
series of tales and legends, pointed and
spiced afresh by his mischievous and thoroughly Provençal wit. Sometimes, in the
midst of the laughter caused by one of
Pistol's stories, the shepherd would say very
gravely, "If a white beard were all that is
needful to be accounted wise, then the goats
would be the wisest." There was also old
Siblet, Dominique, the coachman, and a little
hunchback, called *lou Roudéirou* (the prowler),
a kind of hobgoblin, the spy of the village,
whose sharp, inquisitive glances pierced both
night and walls; an ill-tempered fellow, eaten
up by religious and political hatreds.

You should have heard him imitate and
repeat the stories of old Jean, a red republican of '93, lately dead, and who to the last
remained faithful to his opinions. The
journey of Jean Coste twenty leagues on
foot to go and see his village *curé* and his
two *secondaires* (curates) guillotined. "Ah,
well, my children, when I saw them stick

their heads through the *lunette*—and it was not very becoming to them as a collar—by gad, well, I was pleased ;—*taben aguéré dé plesi.*" Jean Coste all shivering, warming his old carcase against some wall, hot in the blazing sun, and saying to .the lads around him, " Young men, have you read Volney? *Jouven auès legi Veulney ?* He mathematically proved that there is no other God but the sun ! *Gès dé Diou, doum dé Liou ! rèn qué lou souleù !* " And then the way he judged the men of the Revolution: "Marat, good fellow. Saint Just, good fellow. Danton also a good fellow — but towards the end he got spoilt and became moderate in .his views—*dins lou mouderantismo !* " Then the description of Jean Coste's death scene. when, raising himself up like a spectre in his bed, he spoke French for the first time in his life, to throw in the face of the priest : "Avaunt, black raven, the carrion is not yet ready for thee." And the little hunchback

accentuated these last words so horribly that
the women screamed out, "*Aïe!* dear life!"
and the sleeping dogs started awake, and ran
growling towards the door, shaken by the
moaning night wind, until some clear and ringing woman's voice struck up, in order to dispel
the painful impression, a Christmas carol of
Saboly : "*I saw in the air—an angel all green
—with a pair of great
wings — springing   out
from his shoulders;*" or
else the arrival of the
Magi at Bethlehem: *"Be-
hold the Moorish King—
with his rolling eyes;—the
infant Jesus weeps—the
King no longer dares to
enter."* A simple and
flute-like air, that I noted down with all the
imagery, expression and local tradition
gathered up from the ashes of this old hearth.

Often too my fancy carried me off, and I
made little excursions around my windmill.
Sometimes it was a shooting or fishing expedition in Camargue and the pool of Vacarès,
amidst the herds of wild cattle and horses

ranging freely in this pampas-grown °corner.
Another day I went and joined my friends
the Provençal poets, the *Félibres*. At that
time the *Félibrige* had not yet been set up as
an university institution. We were still in
the early days of enthusiasm, in the fervent
and ingenuous stage, devoid of schisms or
rivalry. Five or six jolly comrades, with
innocent child-like laughter and beards like
apostles, met occasionally, either at Maillane,
in Frédéric Mistral's little village, from which
I was separated by the jagged, rocky line of
the Alpilles; or at Arles, in the forum,
surrounded by a throng of drovers and
shepherds gathered together to be hired by
the farmers. Or we went to Aliscamps, and
there, lying on the grass amongst the sarco-
phagi of gray stone, listened to some fine
drama of Théodore Aubanel's, while the air
vibrated with the click of the grasshopper,
and from behind a screen of gray trees,
resounded ironically the blows of the
hammers in the workshops of the Paris-
Lyons-Mediterranean Railway. When the
reading was over, we took a turn on the
Lice, just to see pass, in her white necker-

chief and little helmet-shaped cap, the proud
and coquettish Arlésienne, for whose sake
poor Jan killed himself. At other times our
trysting-place was at the Ville des Baux, that
powdery mass of crumbling ruins, wild rocks
and escutcheoned palaces, which rocked
feebly in the wind, perched up like eagles'
nests on the heights, from whence could be
descried, far beyond the plains, a line of
purer, brighter blue, which is the sea. We
supped at the inn at Cornille; and strolled
about all the evening, singing verses in the
midst of the little winding streets, the tumbled
down walls, the ruined stairways and columns,
all lighted up by a spectral light, which
tipped the grass and stones as with a slight
sprinkling of snow.

"Poets *anén!*" said Master Cornille.
"People who like to see the ruins by
moonlight."

The Félibrige also met amongst the reeds
and rushes of the island of Barthelasse,
opposite the ramparts of Avignon and the
Papal Palace, silent witnesses of the intrigues
and adventures of the little Vedène. Then,
after breakfasting in some little boatman's

tavern, we went up to see the poet Anselme Mathieu, at Châteauneuf-des-Papes, famous for its vines, which for a long time were the most celebrated in Provence. Oh, the wine of the Popes, the golden, regal, imperial, pontifical wine! We drank it up there on the hill, and sang the verses of Mistral, new fragments out of his *Iles d'or.* "At Arles, in the olden times—bloomed the Queen Ponsirade—a rose bush." And then again the fine sea ditty, "The boat comes from Majorca—with a cargo of oranges." What with the blazing sun, the sloping vineyards, propped up by low dry stone walls, the olive, pomegranate and myrtle trees, one might have fancied oneself in Majorca. Through the open casement flew away the rhymes, humming like bees, and we too, carried away by them, spent whole days flitting across the sunny province of Comtat, through highways and byeways, making a halt in the towns, under the plane trees in the

Corso, or the Square; and with much loud-voiced gesticulation, we distributed from our lofty waggonette, nostrums to the assembled populace. Our nostrum was Provençal verse; fine verses in the language of these peasants, who understood and greeted with applause the strophes of *Mireille*, of *la Vénus d'Arles* by Aubanel, a legend of Anselme Mathieu or Roumanille; and took up the chorus with us in the song to the Sun : *Great Sun of Provence,—gay comrade of the mistral, — thou who swallowest up the Durance—like a goblet of Crau wine.* And we wound up with an improvised ball, or dance, the lads and lasses in their working attire; and the corks flying round the tables; and if perchance some prayer-muttering old harridan ventured to criticize the freedom of our mirth, the handsome Mistral,

proud as King David, would say, looking down upon her, "Be quiet, be quiet old mother. Everything is permissible to poets." And he added, confidentially winking to the old woman, who dazzled, respectfully curtsied to him, "*Es nautré qué fasen li saumé.* — It is we who write the psalms."

How delightful it was to return, after one of these lyrical escapades, to the windmill, and lying on the grass of the platform, to think over the book I should sooner or later make out of all this; a book to which I would give the murmur that lingered in my ears, of those songs, that ringing laughter, those fairy-like legends, and also the reflection of that vibrating sun-light, the perfume of those sunburnt hill-sides, and that I would date from my dear ruin with its shattered and useless sails.

The first *Lettres de mon Moulin* appeared, somewhere about 1866, in a Parisian paper where these Provençal chronicles, signed under a double pseudonym borrowed from Balzac "Marie-Gaston," jarred by the peculiarity of their style. Gaston was my

comrade Paul Arène, then a young man,
who had just had a little piece of his,
full of wit and vivacity, played at the Odéon ;
he lived **near me** on the confines of the
woods of Meudon.   But although this
exquisite writer had not **yet** put to his
credit *Jean des Figues*, nor *Paris ingénu*, nor
yet **many pages of his** delicate and powerful
writings, he had already too much real talent,
too strong a personality, to be satisfied for
long with the **mere** occupation of a miller's
man.   I therefore remained alone to fashion
my little stories, at the changing caprice of
each breeze and each hour, while I led a
terribly restless **existence.**   The **work** was
broken and **intermittent ; then I** married,
and **carried off my wife to** Provence, to show
her my windmill.   Nothing had changed
there, neither the landscape nor the welcome.
The **old mother tenderly pressed** us both to
her little checked shawl, and a place was
made for the *novio* **at the boys'** table.   She
sat **by my side on the** platform of the windmill, where the *tramontana*, beholding in this
Parisian an enemy of sunshine and wind,
took pleasure in shaking and ruffling her,

striving to bear her away in a whirlwind like Chénier's young Tarentine.

It was on my return from this journey that, seized again by a love for my Provence, I began in the *Figaro* a new series of *Lettres de mon Moulin, Les Vieux, La Mule du Pape, L'Elixir du Père Gaucher*, &c. ; written at Champrosay, in that studio of Eugène Delacroix's which I have already mentioned in the story of *Jack*, and of *Robert Helmont.* The volume was published by Hetzel, in 1869, two thousand copies were with difficulty disposed of, waiting, like my other earlier works, till the success of my novels should create some further demand for them. Nevertheless it is still my favourite book, not from a literary point of view, but because it recalls the happiest hours of my youth, madcap laughter, intoxication without remorse, friendly faces and places that I shall never see again.

Now Montauban is deserted, the "dear Mamma" is dead, the sons dispersed, the Châteauneuf vineyard utterly destroyed. Where are Miracle and Miraclet, Siblet, Mitifio, le Roudéirou? If I went down

there, I should find no one I knew.   They
tell me however that the pines are very
much grown, and above the glittering un-
dulations of their dark green tops, my
windmill turns merrily round in the sun ;
repaired, recovered, with new sails, like a
vessel just afloat; poet set once more to
the wind ; dreamer restored to life and
action.

MY FIRST PLAY.

AH, how long ago that was! Far, very far
from Paris, I was enjoying a springtide of
happiness, under a flood of light, at the
further end of Algeria in the valley of Chélif,
one fine day in February, 1862. Thirty miles
of plain lay before me, bordered on the right
and left by a double line of mountains, all
transparent and purple like amethysts in the
golden mist. Lentisks dwarf palms, stony
beds of dried torrents, choked with oleanders ;
and far apart in the distance a caravansary or
an Arab village ; on the heights, some saint's
tomb gleaming in its whitewash, like a
great die capped by a half orange, and
hither and thither, under the broad white
expanse of sunlight, dark moving objects,

which are flocks, and which, were it not for
the deep uniform blue of the sky, might
be mistaken for gliding shadows cast by the
passing clouds.   All the morning we had
been hunting; then the afternoon heat
becoming too oppressive, my friend *bachaga*,
Boualem had the tent pitched.   One of the
sides was raised on poles, like an awning;
and from that side the whole horizon was
visible.   In front of us the hobbled horses
stood motionless with their heads down, the
great deer-hounds slept curled up in the sun;
and lying down flat on his stomach in the
midst of his little pots and pans, our coffee
maker was preparing the moka on a tiny fire
of dry twigs, the thin smoke of which
ascended straight up into the air; while we
lay silently rolling big cigarettes,—Boualem-
Ben-Cherifa, his friends Si Sliman, Sid'Omar,
the *aga* of the Atafs and myself, stretched
out on cushions in the shadow of the white
tent, tinted amber by the sunlight outside,
while the outline of the symbolical crescent
and bloody hand, obligatory ornaments of
every Arab dwelling, appeared like trans-
parencies on the canvas.

It was a delicious afternoon, and one which should have lasted for ever! One of those golden hours, which stand out, after even four and twenty years, radiant as on the first day, from the gray background of life. And see how illogical and perverse is our unfortunate human nature. To this day I cannot think of that siesta in the tent, without regret and longing : but on that afternoon I must own, in that country, I thirsted for Paris.

Yes, I regretted Paris, which I had been obliged to leave abruptly on account of my health, seriously impaired by my five years literary novitiate. I regretted Paris for all the beloved reasons I left there behind me : for its fogs and its gas, for its newspapers and new books, for the evening discussions at the café, or under the portico of the theatre, for that glorious fever of art, and that perpetual enthusiasm, of which at that time I only saw the sincere side ; I regretted it above all, on account of my play, my first play !—of which the acceptance at the Odéon had been announced to me on the very day of departure. Certainly, the land-

scape before me was beautiful, and the
setting of it singularly poetic; but I would
then willingly have exchanged Algeria and ,
the Atlas, Boualem and his friends, the blue
of the sky, the gleaming white of the
Marabouts' tombs, and the exquisite pink

of the oleanders, for the
gray colonnade of the
Odéon, the little lobby of
the artists' entrance, and
the office of Constant the
concierge, a man of taste,
—all hung with autographs
of actors and portraits of
actresses   in   costume.
Instead of all this, there I was in Algeria, leading the life of a great lord of medieval times,
when I might have been moving triumphantly,
with the hypocritically modest mien of the new
author whose piece is about to be played,
through those repulsive corridors, which
had once seen me so trembling and timid.
I was accustoming myself to the society of
Arab chiefs, undeniably picturesque, but
wanting in conversation; while the prompter,
the scene-shifters, the manager, the director

and all the innumerable tribe of over-painted
and dyed actresses and blue-chinned actors
were busy over my piece ! I breathed the
fresh and penetrating scent of the breeze-

kissed
orange groves,
when I might have
delighted my nostrils with the
close and fusty odour peculiar to theatre
walls ! And then the ceremony of reading to
the actors, the bottle and tumbler of water,
and the manuscript shining white under
the lamp ! The rehearsals too ! in the

green room at first, round the great chimney piece, then on the stage : the stage,
with its mysterious, unfathomable depths,
all crowded with frame-work and side
scenes, facing the empty house, echoing as a
cavern, and freezing to behold, with the
great chandelier covered up, and the boxes,
dress circle and stalls all shrouded in gray
linen.   Then would come the first representation ; the front of the theatre, casting on
the square before it, the cheerful brightness
of its lines of gas, the vehicles arriving, the
crowd at the box office, the anxious wait at
the café opposite, alone with some faithful
friend, and then the throb of emotion,
striking the heart like a blow, at the moment when shadows in black coats, moving
with animation, appearing against the lighted
windows of the lobby, announced that the
curtain has fallen, and that, amidst applause
or hooting, the name of the author has been pro-
claimed. "Come," says the friend, "courage ;
we must go and see how it has all gone off;
thank the actors, and shake hands with the
friends who are impatiently waiting in the
little room at the café Tabourey."   This

was the dream that I dreamt wide awake beneath the tent, in the drowsy heat of a fine month in the African winter ; whilst far away, amongst the oblique rays of the sunset, a well—white but an hour ago—became rose tinted; and for all noise, on the silence of the vast plain, rose the tinkle of a sheep bell and the melancholy call of the shepherds.

There was absolutely nothing to disturb my reverie. My hosts knew, amongst the four of them, some twenty words of French ; I for my part, scarcely ten words of Arabic. The companion who had brought me there and who usually served as my interpreter (a Spanish corn merchant, whose acquaintance I had made at Milianah) was not with me, having persevered in the chase : so that we smoked our great cigarettes in silence, while sipping the black Moorish coffee out of microscopic cups, inserted in egg-cups of silver filigree.

Suddenly, there was a great commotion, the dogs barked, the servants ran hither and thither, a great long devil of a spahi in his red burnous stopped his horse short in front of the tent and said,—" Sidi Daoudi ? "

It was a telegram from Paris, which had
followed my track from camp to camp since
I left Milianah. It contained merely these
words :—" Piece played yesterday, great
success, Rousseil and Tisserant splendid !

I read and re-read this delightful
telegram, twenty times, a hundred
times over, as if it were a love letter. Only
think ! my first piece. Seeing my hands
trembling with emotion, and the happiness
shining in my eyes, the " agas " smiled at me

and spoke among themselves in Arabic. The
cleverest of them even called up all his learn-

ing to his aid, in order to say to me,
" France—news—family ? " Ah no, it was no
news of my family which made my heart beat

so rapturously; and unable to accustom myself to the notion of having no one to whom
I could communicate my delight, I set to
work to explain with my four words of Arabic
and the twenty words of French I believed
them to understand, what a theatre was, and
the importance of a first representation in
Paris, to the aga of the Atafs, to Sid'Omar,
to Si-Sliman, and Boualem Ben-Cherifa. Hard
work, as you may fancy ! I hunted for com-
parisons, I expressed myself in endless
pantomime, I flourished the blue cover of the
telegram saying : Karagueuz ! Karagueuz ! as
if my affecting little piece, intended to touch
the heart and draw forth tears from the eyes
of innocence, could possibly have any affinity
with the monstrous and devilish buffoonery in
which the Turks delight ; and as if one could
without blasphemy compare the classic
Odéon with the clandestine haunts of every
Moorish town, in which at night, notwithstanding the exertions of the police, the good Mus-
sulmans assemble to enjoy the spectacle of the
wanton adventures of their favourite hero!

These are the mirages of Africa. In Paris a
disappointment awaited me. For I returned to

Paris at once in frantic haste, and much
sooner than prudence and the doctors would
sanction. But what mattered to me the fog
and the snow that I sought, what did I care
for the balmy sky I should leave behind me?
To see my piece! Nothing else in the world
signified. I am on board, I am on shore, I
fly through Marseilles, and behold me in the
train, trembling with eager excitement. I
arrived in Paris at about six o'clock in the
evening, when it was dark. I could not wait
for dinner, but cried: " To the Odéon,
Cabby!" Ah, youth! youth!   .

They were about to draw up the curtain
when I seated myself in my stall. The house
presented a strange appearance; it was Shrove
Tuesday; there would be dancing all night at
Bullier, and a large number of students and
their sweethearts had come to pass a couple
of hours at the play in their masquerade
costumes. There were jesters, clowns,
pierrots, pierrettes, follies. " Difficult, very
difficult," I thought to myself, " to bring tears
to the eyes of such a motley crowd!"
They did cry however, and cried so much
that the spangles on the dresses, which

H

caught the light, seemed so many bright
tear-drops.   On my right was a little Folly
whose cap and bells were shaken every moment by her sobs, and on my left a Pierrette,
a fat, roundabout creature with a tender heart,
absurd to see in her emotion, with two great
streams running from her eyes and falling
down the double furrow coursed in the powder on her cheeks.   Decidedly, the telegram
had not lied, my little piece really was a great
success.   During this time however I, the
author, would gladly have been a hundred
feet under ground.   The play that these
good people were applauding, I now considered odiously bad.   What a failure!   Was
that my dream? that fat man, who, in order
to appear paternal and virtuous, had made
himself up to resemble Béranger!   Naturally,
I was most unjust : Tisserant and Rousseil,
two artists of great ability, acted as well as
an actor can act, and to their talent was due
much of my success.   But the blow was
terrible, the difference too monstrous between
that which I fancied I had written, and what
I now saw before me ; showing all its flaws,
blemishes and defects in the pitiless glare of

the footlights; and cruelly I suffered on seeing my cherished ideal reduced to a mere stuffed lay figure. Notwithstanding the emotion, notwithstanding the applause, I felt an indescribable sensation of shame and disgust. The blood rushed hotly to my head and flushed my cheeks. It seemed to me as if all this masquerading public were scoffing at me and knew me. Wretched, ill, losing my head, I nervously repeated the actor's gestures. I longed to make them move more quickly, speak more quickly, skim over phrases and stage, so that the torture might be the sooner ended. What a relief it was when the curtain fell, and I could make my escape, skirting the walls, with turned up coat-collar, shamefaced and stealthy as a thief.

HENRI ROCHEFORT.

SOMEWHERE about 1859, I made the acquaintance of an excellent fellow, who was one of the clerks in the *bureaux* of the Hôtel de Ville. His name was Henri Rochefort, but this name at that time conveyed no particular meaning. Rochefort lived in a quiet and unpretending manner with his parents in the old rue des Deux-Boules, within reach of his work, in the swarming Quartier Saint-Denis, invaded by business and fancy goods, with its houses full of shops, covered from top to

bottom with sign-boards, everywhere samples
displayed, placards hung at the sides of the
doors : such as, *Feathers and flowers, Imi-
tation Jewellery, Beads and Spangles, Mock
Pearls;* a different trade on every floor; a
perpetual noise of work descending from
the windows to the street below; vans being
loaded, parcels tied up, clerks running about
pen behind ear; a work-girl in her smock,
gilt-clips sticking in her hair; and here and
there some fine old mansion turned into a
wholesale shop, its coat-of-arms and sculp-
tures carrying one's thoughts back a couple
of centuries, causing one to dream of upstart
valets, financiers made of money, of Count
Horn, of the Regent, of the Mississippi, of
Law and his great scheme; of the time, in
short, when in these now commercial and
bourgeois streets fluctuated the most wildly
impossible fortunes; a flood of feverish
excitement and of wealth rolling with the
majestic impassibility of a tide from out of
that narrow, stinking passage hard by, still
called rue Quincampoix ! My friend Rochefort was a little like the street he lived in,
and held his past in small account. Every

one knew he was of noble birth, son of a
Count; he appeared to ignore that, and
simply called himself Rochefort; and this
American simplicity did not fail to impress
me, freshly imported from our vain and
legitimist South.

M. de Rochefort, the father, belonged to
the generation of men who were young in
1830, and whose career was interrupted and
future spoilt by the Revolution of July. It was
a particularly amiable and witty generation,
preserving a delicate perfume of *ancien régime*
in the atmosphere of Louis Philippe's reign;
sulking at the new royalty, without however
sulking at France; attached to the elder
branch, but too well aware that any res-
toration must be for a long time impossible
to permit the slightest mark of the gloomy
temper of the fanatic or sectarian to brand
their sceptical and disinterested loyalty. While
some of them amused themselves by bom-
barding the Tuileries with their sparkling wit,
or protested against the dulness of the *bourgeois* manners by joining the uproarious crowd
of masqueraders and jingling jesters, in the
legendary " descente de la Courtille "; others

less scatterbrained or poorer, tried to procure
by their own labour what they could no longer
hope for from the good graces of royalty. Thus
did M. de Lauzanne, whom we saw not long
ago pass by still brisk and smiling, still erect
in spite of his great age, still a thorough gentleman, notwithstanding his work as a vaudevilliste, and the nickname of Father Lauzanne
which his colleagues with affectionate familiarity bestowed on him ; thus did also M.
de Rochefort, who in his day had been the
intimate friend of the ex-bodyguard "Choca,"
and very prominent in his time among the
noisy young royalist party.   Having been
much addicted to haunting the green room,
Rochefort, the father, like Lauzanne, when
bad times came, remembered the way to the
theatre, and returned thither, this time to
make a livelihood.   Within every amateur
is concealed an author ; and from applauding
plays, to trying to write them, the transition
is easy ; thus M. de Rochefort-Luçay wrote
plays and became a vaudevilliste.

These details are not without meaning, for
they serve to give us an idea of the surroundings in which Rochefort's childhood was

passed. It was a curious childhood, characteristic and very Parisian, spent entirely between
the Lycée and the little world of the theatre ;

the cafés to which his father took him on
Sundays, where authors and actors meet, are
more patriarchal than is generally supposed ;
and instead of the mad revels dreamt of by

the provincial mind, one hears the dry click
of the dice thrown on the backgammon boards,
or of the dominoes as they are moved to and
fro.   Rochefort was therefore the collegian,
son of an artist or man of letters, that we
have all known, initiated from childhood into
the secrets of the green room, addressing the
most celebrated actors with familiarity, knowing all about the newest plays, secretly giving
orders for the play to the under master, and
thus able to compose with impunity in the
recesses of his desk, in company with a pipe
and a tame lizard, a whole heap of master-
pieces, dramatic or otherwise, which he would
carry on the next holiday, his cap jauntily
stuck aside, and his heart beating fiercely
enough to burst the buttons off his tunic, —
to the letter-boxes—never open—of the
newspaper offices, or to the sneering stage
doorkeepers of the theatres.   The destiny of
such collegians can be traced beforehand : at
twenty they obtain a clerkship of some sort,
ministerial or civil, and continue to manufacture subterranean literature at the bottom
of a desk, concealing it from their chiefs as
they had done from their schoolmasters.

H 2

Rochefort did not escape the usual fate. After
trying the highest flights of literature, and
after having fruitlessly sent I know not how
many odes and sonnets to all the poetic
assemblies of France, he used, when I knew
him, the pens and paper of the Paris Munici-
pality in writing short *résumés* of plays for
the *Charivari,* which was just then reforming
its staff and trying to infuse therein a little
fresh blood.

Although I could not guess the future in
store for Rochefort, his physiognomy interested me from the very first. It was evidently
not that of a man who would long put up
with this clerk-like existence, fettered by the
punctuality of the office hours, as exasperating
as the tic-tac of a Black Forest cuckoo clock.
You know the strange head, just such as it
has always remained, a head of hair standing
erect and bristly above a forehead almost too
large, at one and the same time an abode for
neuralgia and a reservoir of enthusiasm ;
deep and hollow eyes gleaming under the
shadow of the brow, the nose, straight and
sharp, the mouth curved bitterly, the whole
face lengthened by a pointed beard, which

inevitably made one think of a sceptical
Don Quixote, or a gentle Mephistopheles.
Very thin, he wore a wretched black coat,
which was much too tight, and it was his
custom to keep his hands buried in his
trouser pockets—a deplorable habit, which
made him seem even thinner than he really
was, accentuating terribly the angularity of
his elbows and the narrowness of his
shoulders.   He was generous and a good
friend, capable of great self sacrifice, and
under the appearance of coldness, was
nervous and easily irritated.   One day, in
consequence of an article, on what subject I
no longer remember, he had a duel with the
editor of the *Gaulois* newspaper.   The *Gaulois* of that day (for the title of a newspaper
in France has more incarnations than Buddha,
and passes through more hands than the
betrothed of the King of Garbe), the *Gaulois*
of that day, was one of those ephemeral
cabbage leaves such as spring up between the
paving stones around the cafés of the theatres
and the literary taverns.   The editor, a short,
jolly, witty, red and round little man, was,
as far as I can recollect, called Delvaille

and signed himself Delbrecht, no doubt
thinking that a prettier name. Delvaille or
Delbrecht, whichever you please, had pro-
voked Rochefort. Rochefort would have pre-
ferred to fight with pistols; not that he was
a very alarmingly good shot, but he had
sometimes won a few macaroons at a fair:
while, as to a sword, neither from far nor
from near, could he ever remember having
seen such a thing. Delvaille, having been
challenged, had choice of weapons, and chose
swords. "Very well then, said Rochefort, I
will fight with swords." A rehearsal of the
duel was held in Paul Véron's room. Rochefort was willing to run the risk of being
killed, but not that of appearing ridiculous.
Véron therefore had summoned a great
sergeant-major of Zouaves (since then cut to
pieces at Solferino) very skilful at the salutes,
attitudes, and manners most in fashion in the
barrack fencing school. "After you—Not
at all—To please you—Proceed, Sir."
After ten minutes fencing, Rochefort might
as far as grace went, have shown the most
moustached *la Ramée* how to set to work.
The two champions met the next day, in those

delightful woods of Chaville between Paris
and Versailles, which we all know so well,
often spending Sunday there in less warlike
pastimes. A cold fine rain was falling that
day, making bubbles on the pond, and veiling
in a faint mist the green circle of hills, the
slope of a ploughed field, and the fallen sides
of a red sand pit. The combatants took off
their shirts, notwithstanding the rain, and,
but for the gravity of the situation, one would
have been tempted to laugh at seeing, face to
face, this little fat and white-haired fellow,
in a flannel vest piped with blue at the wrists,
putting himself into position as correctly as
on the platform ; and Rochefort, lanky, spare,
yellow, grim as a death's head, and so cased
in bony ribs that one really doubted whether
there was space upon his body for the prick
of a sword. Unfortunately, he had forgotten
in the night all the fine lessons of the sergeant-
major, held his sword like a taper and made
the most reckless thrusts leaving himself
exposed. At the first pass he received a
thrust which grazed his side. The sword
had scratched him but very slightly. It was
his first duel.

I shall surprise no one by saying that even
then Rochefort was witty; but it was a

kind of concentrated wit, of subtle essence
consisting, above all, of cutting words long
meditated, in the association of ideas utterly

incongruous and unforeseen ; in the wildest
absurdities, in chilling, and ferocious jokes,
which he muttered between his teeth with the
voice of Cham, and the silent laugh of
Leather-stocking.   But this wit remained
useless and congealed. His witticisms were
amusing enough when uttered among intimate friends and comrades, but to write and
print such things, to plunge into literature
with any such furious bounds and capers,
appeared impossible.   Rochefort did not
know his own value, and as is generally the
case, it was a chance, an accident, which
revealed to him his talent. He had for
friend and inseparable companion, a singular
figure, whose mere name will raise a smile
amongst those of my own generation who
can recall an acquaintance with him.   He
was called Léon Rossignol.   A true type
of old man's child, one might almost say he
was born old.   Slim and blanched like a
lettuce grown in a cellar, at eighteen he was
a confirmed snuff-taker, coughed and ex-
pectorated, and leant with an air of dignity
on a stick worthy of a grandpapa.   A medley
of irreconcilable elements ; or rather having

in him some unsettled spirit, this bold fellow,
strange to say, was fond of a quarrel and
afraid of a blow.   Cowardly and insolent as
Panurge, he was capable of provoking without rhyme or reason the first carabineer he
met in the street, and if the soldier took
the joke amiss—of falling on his knees to
beg pardon, with such exaggerated humility,
that the offended party scarcely knew
whether to laugh or be angry.   In short, he
was a grown-up child, weak and sickly;
beloved by Rochefort on account of his ready
command of vulgar oratory, wittily attuned to
the taste of the populace, and whom he
saved more than once from the consequences
he might have brought upon himself through
some practical joke carried too far. Rossignol,
like Rochefort, was employed at the Hôtel
de Ville.   He was perched aloft, on the top
story, under the roof, in an office, far away
at the end of a labyrinth of narrow staircases
and passages, and there, in charge of stores,
he gravely distributed as required, paper,
pens, pencils, pen-knives, letter-weights,
squares of india-rubber, bottles of pounce
powder, blue ink, red ink, gold dust, illustrated

almanacs, and I know not what else ; all the
useless paraphernalia with which the idle
penmen of a great office love to surround
themselves, and which one may call the flora
of office life. Rossignol too had naturally
literary ambition. To see his name in some
publication or another was his most ardent
desire, and we used to amuse ourselves,
Pierre Véron, Rochefort and I, by cooking
up for him scraps of articles, or improvising
little quatrains, which he at once carried, full
of pride, to the *Tintamarre*. This irrespon-
sibility had a curious effect. Rochefort, who,
when he wrote under his own name was
hampered by servile imitations and con-
ventionalism, showed originality and individuality the moment he wrote under the
signature of Rossignol. Then he was free,
then he did not feel the irritated eye of the
Institute following on his paper the un-
academic contortions of his thought and
style. And it was delightful to see this bold
spirit indulging in mirth ; cool, incisive, full of
astonishing audacity and familiarity, with
a feeling peculiar to himself for everything
pertaining to Parisian life, and for taking it as

text for all manner of jokes, put together with
patience and without mercy; in the midst
of which the phrase maintained the solemnity
of a clown between two grins, content with

just one wink, when once the paragraph
was ended.

"But this is charming, new, original, quite
yourself; why don't you write like this on
your own account?" "You are right perhaps.
I must try." Rochefort's style was dis-

covered, the Empire had now to look to itself.

It has been said that it was the spirit of Arnal on paper, and that Rochefort had only put in paragraphs the dialogues of Duvert and Lauzanne. We do not deny the influence. It is evident that the point of view and the mode of expressing in a set formula a given proceeding, of turning the dialogue and giving a fanciful twist to the thought, which, during the endless games of dominoes on the Boulevard du Temple, had made an impression on his school-boy brain, were not without their use to him afterwards. But these are unconscious imitations, from which no one can escape. It is not contrary to the laws of literature to pick up a rusty weapon; the important part is to know how to sharpen the blade, and to re-model the hilt to the measure of one's hand.

Rochefort made his *début* in the *Nain Jaune,* edited by Aurélien Scholl. Who does not know Scholl? However little you may have frequented the Boulevards of Paris, or visited their neighbourhood during the last thirty years, you must have remarked in front of Tortoni's, under the lime trees of Baden,

or the palms of Monte Carlo, these pre-
eminently Parisian and Boulevardier features.
By the gaiety of the accent, the clear sharp-
ness of the tone, the brilliant and trenchant
sparkle of the style, Scholl—in the midst of
a Paris overwhelmed by Parliamentary slang
and the foolish babble of reporters—remains
one of the last, we might almost say *the* last,
petit journaliste. The *petit journaliste* in the
sense given to the words, means a journalist
who thinks himself bound to be at the same
time a journalist and a good writer; the great
journalist considers himself free from this
obligation.   Like many others, in these
troubled latter days, Scholl, little by little,
seeing no harm in it, has been drawn into the
political arena.   He is in the full heat of the
battle now, and it is amusing to see this
grandson of Rivarol become republican,
pointing against the enemies of the Republic, the golden arrows dipped in a little
poison, borrowed from the reactionary arsenal
of the *Actes des Apôtres.*   But at the date of
the *Nain Jaune,* politics languished, and
neither did Scholl any more than Rochefort have any thought or expectation of a

Republic. He contented himself with being one of the most amiable sceptics and the wittiest scoffers in Paris. Passionately fond of display, in his character of Bordelais, he maintained—what in those good old times of *Sainte Bohême* had a faint suspicion of paradox about it—he maintained that a literary man ought to pay his bootmaker, and that one could be witty and yet own fresh gloves and a clean shirt. Faithful to his principles, he made use of all the elegances of the moment, even to the eye glass wedged in the corner of his eye, to which he still adheres; he breakfasted at Bignon's, and afforded the Parisians the entirely novel sight of a simple chronicler partaking daily of his boiled egg and his cutlet, in company with the Duc de Grammont-Caderousse, who was at that time the reigning monarch of the gilded youth. The *Nain Jaune* was the only serious rival Villemessant ever encountered. Greatly helped forward by his fashionable acquaintances, Scholl, in a few months had succeeded in making his journal the organ of high life, and of the clubs, the umpire of Parisian elegance; but, at the end of a year, he

became disgusted, and thought himself worthy
of better things; he was too much of a writer,
too much of a journalist, to remain long as
a mere editor.

Rochefort's success in the *Nain Jaune* was
rapid, and in the *Figaro*, which hastened to
secure his pen, he was still more brilliant.
The Parisians, always critical fault-finders,
and long unaccustomed to independence
took a fancy to these pamphlets, which set
to work to mock aloud, in a tone of jeering
raillery, all sorts of solemn and official things
which, till now, the boldest had hardly dared
to jest at in a whisper.   Rochefort was fairly
launched, he had duels, more successful than
that on the borders of the pond at Chaville ;
he gambled, lived generously, filled Paris with
the noise of his fame, and remained, in spite
of all, notwithstanding the intoxication of the
successes of an evening or an hour, the same
Rochefort I had known at the Hôtel de Ville,
always modest and kindly, always ready to do
a service to a friend; always uneasy about
the forthcoming article, always fearing he had
lost the vein, exhausted himself, and could
continue no longer.

Villemessant, who loved to be despotic with his contributors, had for this one an admiration coupled with fear. The mocking and impassive face, the headstrong and fantastic temperament astounded him. The fact is, Rochefort was full of strange obstinacies and singular caprices. I have related elsewhere the effect of his article on M. de Saint Rémy's play, and with what insolent familiarity he put down the pretensions of this unlucky ducal, presidential volume, which had been decked with every term of flattery by each Dangeau and Jules Lecomte of journalism. Paris chuckled at the audacity, Morny felt the hit and called out. With a simplicity worthy of a wounded author, astonishing however on the part of a man of wit, he sent his dramatic works to Jouvin, concluding that Jouvin would have better taste than Rochefort, and that he would write in the *Figaro*, an article which should make amends.

Jouvin accepted the volume, but wrote no article, and the poor Duke had to swallow as best he could, the bitter prose of Rochefort. What happened then appeared incredible and unlikely at first sight, yet it was after all true to human nature. Morny, courted, flattered and all-powerful, conceived a sort of affection, mingled with fear and spite, for the man who had not feared to hold him up to ridicule.

He would have liked to see and know him, to have a quiet explanation with him in a corner, as between two friends. His little court did their best to prove that Rochefort possessed neither wit nor style, and that his judgment was absolutely without weight.

His flatterers (a Vice-Emperor always has plenty of them) visited the quays, and collected little *vaudevilles*, peccadilloes of Rochefort's youth, analysed them, picked them to pieces, and upheld by a thousand conclusive arguments that those of M. de Saint Remy were better. Imaginary crimes were attributed to Rochefort. A fanatical Prudhomme arrived one day at a hand gallop, scarlet with indignation, his eyes starting out of his head. "You know, Rochefort, the famous Rochefort, who gives himself such immaculate airs? Well, do you know what we have found out about him? He was granted a scholarship under the Empire!" What a base and vile

heart the man must have had, who, having
been Imperial scholar at eight years of age,
at thirty declared the plays written by *M. le
Duc* to be contemptible ! A little more and
they would have held Rochefort accountable
for the political opinions of his nurse ! Vain
efforts ; useless revelations. Morny, like a
neglected lover, only became more obstinately
determined to make Rochefort his friend.

The caprice became a mania, which possessed him all the more that Rochefort, made
aware of it, practised a sort of comic coquetry
in persistently refusing to know the Duke.
How well I remember, at the first representation of the *Belle Hélène*, Morny stopping
Villemessant in the lobby, saying : "This
time, you must introduce Rochefort to me !"
" Monsieur le Duc ! Certainly, Monsieur le
Duc ! It was but a moment since that we
were talking about—" And Villemessant ran
off after Rochefort, but Rochefort had vanished. Then the idea was suggested that some
arrangement, some kind of trap should be
laid, by which the Duke and Rochefort should
accidentally be brought together face to face.
The latter was known to be a great collector

of old curios (for had he not published the *Petits Mystères de l'Hôtel des Ventes ?*), and was passionately fond of pictures. The Duke had a good many fine paintings. Rochefort would be induced to come and see the gallery, the Duke would be there, as if by chance, and the introduction would thus take place. A day was fixed, a friend undertook to bring Rochefort ; the Duke waited in his picture gallery ; he waited one hour, two hours, alone with his Rembrandts and his Hobbemas, and again this time the wished-for monster never came.

While the Duke lived (no doubt by a mere coincidence, for I do not suppose that this distant and unrequited friendship was ever carried to the extent of protecting the ungrateful pamphleteer from the decrees of justice), nevertheless, while the Duke lived, Rochefort was comparatively little molested. But once Morny had disappeared from the scene, the persecutions began. Rochefort, exasperated, redoubled in insolence and audacity. Fines fell as thickly as hailstones, and imprisonment followed up the fines. The censor began to notice his writings.

The censor's conventional palate found that all Rochefort's writings had a strong political flavour. The *Figaro's* very existence was threatened, and Rochefort compelled to withdraw from the paper. He thereupon founded the *Lanterne*, unmasked his batteries, and boldly ran up his pirate flag. It was again Villemessant, Villemessant the conservative, Villemessant of the magisterial fasces, who chartered this fire-ship. The censor and Villemessant on this occasion rendered a strange kind of service to conservatism and to the Empire. The history of the *Lanterne*, and its wonderful success, is well known, the little flame-coloured paper seen in every hand, in the streets, the cabs, the railway carriages, all bright with the red sparks; the Government losing its head, the scandal, the trial, and—inevitable, easily foreseen result—Rochefort named deputy for Paris.

There again, Rochefort remained the same as ever; he carried with him to the benches of the Chamber, even to the tribune, the insulting familiarity of his pamphlets, and to the very last refused to treat the Empire as a

serious adversary.   Do you remember the
scandal?   A government orator, speaking in
a high and mighty tone, and with all the

contempt that a stiff and pompous parliamentary man may feel towards a mere newspaper scribbler, had coupled his name with

the word ridiculous! Pale, with his teeth
clenched, Rochefort rose from his seat, and
smiting the sovereign's cheek, over the
shoulder of his minister said : " I may sometimes have been ridiculous, but I have never
been seen in the tawdry masquerading get-up
of a mountebank dentist, with an eagle on
my shoulder and a piece of fat bacon in my
hat !" That day M. Schneider was presiding.
I can remember the consternation expressed
on his great good-natured face. And picturing
to myself in his place, the Duc de Morny's
refined and haughty face, with its cool and
ironical expression, I said to myself, " What
a pity he is not sitting up there, he would at
last have realized his wish, and made the
acquaintance of Rochefort."

Since then, I have only twice caught sight
of Rochefort : the first time at the funeral of
Victor Noir, fainting and borne past in a cab,
worn out by the desperate struggle of two
hours, that he had maintained by the side of
Delescluze against a bewildered mob of two

hundred thousand unarmed men, who with
women and children insisted on taking back
the body to Paris, and so march on to certain
butchery—as Rochefort knew that cannons
were there, ready to fire on them. Then,
again another time during the war, in the
scurry and bustle of the battle of Buzenval,
with the tramping of the troops, the dull
sound of the cannons in the forts, the
rumbling of the ambulance carts, amid the
fever and the smoke ; bishops showing off on
horseback, fancifully dressed up like masqueraders; brave citizens going off to be
killed, fully believing in Trochu's plan ; in
the midst of the heroic, in the midst of the
grotesque, in the midst of this never-to-be-for-
gotten drama—full as those of Shakespeare
of both the sublime and the ridiculous—
called the Siege of Paris. It was on the road
to Mont Valérien, cold and muddy, the
bare trees shivered sadly against the monotonous gray of the misty sky. My friend
passed by in a carriage, pale and livid as
ever, behind the window; still as in the far-
away days at the Hôtel de Ville, buttoned up
in a tight black coat. I cried to him

through the storm, "Good morning, Rochefort."

Since then I have never seen him again.[1]

---

[1] This description of Rochefort was published in the *Nouveau Temps* of St. Petersburg, in 1879.

HENRY MONNIER.

ONCE more I see myself in the humble garret of my youthful days, in the depth of winter, no fire in the grate, and the window panes clouded by the thick hoar frost. Seated in front of a little white wooden table, my legs wrapped in a travelling rug, I was busily engaged in penning verses. Some one raps at the door,—"Come in!" and in the open doorway a strange apparition comes into sight. Imagine a vast and rotund waistcoat, a shirt collar, a homely, ruddy, close-shaven countenance, with a pair of spectacles astride on a Roman nose. The individual bows ceremoniously, and says,

"I am Henry Monnier."

Henry **Monnier** ; at that time a celebrity !
Actor, writer, artist **in** one, he was pointed
out as he **passed** through the streets, and
M. de Balzac, **the great observer, held him in**
high esteem **for his powers of** observation.
It was a singular style of observation, **it must**
be added, and not at **all that of ordinary**
mortals. Many a writer, **indeed, has acquired**
wealth and renown by rallying **the foibles and**
infirmities of **others.** Monnier however had
not gone far in search of a model : he placed
himself **in front of his** looking-glass, listened
to his own thoughts and words, and finding
the type **thus before** him a profoundly
ridiculous **one, he** conceived that **pitiless**
incarnation, that cruel satire on **the French**
bourgeois, which is known under **the name of**
Joseph Prudhomme. **For Monnier is Joseph**
Prudhomme, **and Joseph Prudhomme is**
Monnier. **From the white gaiters to the**
cravat of many **folds and endless** windings,
they have **all in common. Both** have the
same pompous and turkey-cock style of frill,
the same air of grotesque solemnity, the same
domineering round-eyed stare through the
gold-rimmed spectacles, the **same** impossible

I

apophthegms, delivered in the voice of a
vulture with a cold in the head. "If I
could only get out of my own skin for an
hour or two," says Fantasio to his friend
Spark, "if I could only become that man
passing by!" Monnier, who had but little affinity
with Fantasio, never had any wish to become
that passer-by; possessing in the highest
degree the singular quality of duality, he
sometimes quitted the husk that enveloped
him, in order to turn it into ridicule; and to
laugh at his own appearance; but he soon
wrapped himself again in his cherished
personality, and the relentless scoffer, the
cruel mocker, the scourge of *bourgeois* fool-
ishness, became again in private life the most
ingenuously stupid of the class he ridiculed.

Among other pre-occupations, worthy indeed of Joseph Prudhomme, Henry Monnier
was possessed with one idea, which he held
in common with every provincial magistrate
who is given to improvising rhymes, and with
all the superannuated colonels who employ
their enforced leisure in translating Horace.
He longed to soar aloft on Pegasus, to wear
the buskin and sandals of Thalia, to stoop

and gather in the hollow of his hand—even
at the risk of snapping his mental braces—
some of the pure water of Hippocrene ; he
dreamt of verdant laurels, of academic prizes,
and last, but not least, of seeing a play of his
own acted at the Théâtre
Français. Already—does
any one remember it now ?
—a play of his, in three
acts and in verse, as the
play-bills say, had been
represented at the Odéon ;
Peintres et Bourgeois was
its title : and it was his joint
production with a young
commercial traveller, I
think, who was somewhat
of an expert in the art of
turning a couplet. The
Odéon was all very well ;
but the Théâtre Français !
the home of Molière ! And for twenty
years, Henry Monnier prowled round the
abode of fame, haunting the Café de la
Régence, and the Café Minerve ; wherever
the *sociétaires* of the theatre met together

there Monnier was to be seen, always dignified and trim, his tidy and close-shaven face,
like that of the "noble father" of a play, and
with the conscious .self-satisfied look of a
pedantic exponent of comedy.

The worthy fellow had read my verses, and
counted on my help
to realize his ambi-
tious dreams.   It
was   in   order   to
propose our working
together that he had
clambered panting
up the innumerable
and steep stairs
which led to my
attic in the Rue de
Tournon. You will
easily   understand
how flattered I was,
and with what alacrity I accepted his offer!

The very next day I went to his house.
He occupied, in a respectable-looking old
house in the Rue Ventadour, a small apartment, which bore the very characteristic
stamp of an economical, tidy, fidgety spirit,

at once actor and old bachelor. Everything
—furniture **and** floors—was polished and
shining. In front of each chair was **a little**
round **bit** of carpet, edged with **red cloth,**
neatly pinked out. **There were four** spit-
toons; one in each **corner.** On the mantel-
piece were two saucers, each containing a few
pinches of dry snuff. Monnier occasionally
dipped into them, but never offered any.

The first impression this house conveyed
to my mind **was** that of miserliness. **Later**
on I learnt that this parsimonious appearance
hid **in** reality a **very** hard and difficult life.
Monnier was entirely without fortune : from
time to time the representation of a play, a
short article, the sale **of a few** sketches, came
to supplement, and **that** in a **very** partial
manner, his small resources. Little by little
he had slipped into the habit of dining out
every day. He was a favourite guest, and
paid his welcome by relating, **or** rather acting
—for his parodies and jokes were never
spontaneous—highly seasoned stories after
dinner. They were either some thoroughly
scandalous dialogue between two persons
whose voice he mimicked, or else he repre-

sented his favourite hero, Monsieur Prudhomme, carrying his great stomach and his
imperturbable solemnity through the most
doubtful and ticklish adventures. All this
was delivered without a smile; for the
bourgeois lurking within Henry Monnier
secretly rebelled at playing the part of
buffoon. He was full too of despotic and
unreasonable requirements; insisting, for
instance, on a quarter of an hour's nap after
dinner, no matter how high the society in
which he happened to be; and was seized with
fits of jealousy, sullenness, and rage, like an
old parrot robbed of the bone he is picking,
if by chance any other than himself led the
conversation at table, and threatened to put
him in the shade. At one time his friends
were anxious to obtain for him a government
pension; it would have seemed wealth to
the poor fellow, but in this instance his after-
dinner jokes had an unfortunate effect.
Malassis had published a collection of his
stories in Belgium; a copy was sent over to
Paris, the ministerial propriety was declared
to be outraged, and the promised pension
vanished into thin air. This volume must

not be mistaken for the *Bas fonds de Paris*,
which by comparison might have been written
for young girls ; although the publication of
even this last was only permitted on suffer-
ance, and restricted to a very limited number
of copies, sufficiently expensive to prevent
the volume from exerting a dangerous influence beyond the excommunicated frontiers
of the world of bibliophiles.

Such was the double nature of this man—
homo duplex—who did me the honour of
wishing to make me partner in his literary
work. Full as I was at twenty of whimsical
fancy, I might have been able to agree with
the buffoon, but unfortunately it was the
bourgeois Prudhomme, and he alone, who
wished to collaborate with me. After a few
interviews I ceased my visits to him. No
doubt Henry Monnier hardly regretted me ;
and of my first dream of fame nothing
remains but the memory of this ridiculous
old man in his neat and shabby home,
taking little whiffs out of little pipes, and
seated in the leather arm-chair, wherein he was
found dead one morning some fifteen years ago.

THE END OF A MERRY-ANDREW,

AND OF MURGER'S BOHEMIA.

WHEN I was about eighteen, I made the acquaintance of a somewhat singular individual, who now seems to me, after a certain lapse of time, to be the very personification of a world to itself, with special language and peculiar manners, a world that has disappeared and is now almost forgotten ; but which at one time held a prominent place in the Paris of the Empire. I allude to that gipsy band, guerillas of art, rebels against conventional philosophy and literature, fantastic to the very uttermost, which had insolently ensconced itself before the Louvre and the Institute, and which Henri Murger —not without embellishing and poetizing the remembrance of it—has celebrated under the title of *Bohemia.* We will call my personage Desroches. I had met him at a ball of the Quartier Latin, with some friends, one summer evening. I had returned home very late to my little room in the Rue de Tournon, and was sleeping as soundly as a dormouse the next morning, when suddenly there appeared, at the foot of my bed, a man in a black coat, a scanty, threadbare coat, of that peculiar black only seen on policemen and undertakers.

· "I come from M. Desroches."

"M. Desroches? What M. Desroches?" said I, rubbing my eyes, for my recollections that morning obstinately refused to be aroused as quickly as my body.

"M. Desroches of the *Figaro.* You spent the evening together last night ; he is in the lock-up, and he refers to you."

"M. Desroches—ah, to be sure—

I 2

exactly—he refers to me—well, tell them to let
him out!"

"Beg pardon, there is fifteen-pence to
pay!"

"Fifteen-pence! Why?"

"It is the custom."

I gave the fifteen-pence. The black-coated
man disappeared, and I remained sitting on
my bed, half dreaming, and not clearly under-
standing in consequence of what eccentric
adventures I found myself brought to the
point of ransoming, like a new brother of
mercy—for fifteen-pence—a contributor to
the *Figaro* from the clutches not of the Turks,
but of the police.

I had no long time for reflection. Five
minutes later, Desroches, freed from his
fetters, came smiling into my room.

"A thousand pardons, my dear colleague;
all this is the fault of the *Raisins muscats.*
Yes! the *Raisins muscats,* my first article,
which appeared yesterday in the *Figaro.*
Confounded *Raisins muscats!* You see, I
had got the payment—my first payment
—and it flew to my head. We patrolled
the whole quarter after we left you, indeed

towards the end my recollections are somewhat mixed; still I have a sensation as if
I had received a kick somewhere or another.
Then I found myself in the station-
house—a charming night indeed! First

of all they poked me into the furthest
den—the black hole, you know. How it
smelt! But I made the gentlemen laugh
—they were good enough to take me into
their guard-room—we talked, played cards

They insisted on my reading them *les
Raisins muscats*, such a success! . . . It is
really astonishing the taste these policemen
have!"

Imagine my stupefaction, and the effect
produced on my simple and provincial boyish
mind by the revelation of these eccentric
literary habits and customs! And the
colleague who thus related his adventures
was a little round fellow, well brushed and
shaved, affecting polite manners, and whose
white gaiters and frock coat of *bourgeois* cut
made the most marked contrast with his
extravagant gestures and the grimaces of his
buffoon-like features. He astonished me,
half frightened me, saw that he did so, and
evidently took pleasure in exaggerating, in
honour of me, the cynicism of his paradoxes.

"I like you," he said, as he took his leave;
"come and see me next Sunday afternoon.
I live in a delightful spot, near the Castle
of Fogs, on the hillside looking over Saint-
Ouen, you know it well—the vineyard of
Gérard de Nerval! I will introduce you
to my wife; she's worth taking a journey to
see. Happily, too, I have just received a

barrel of new wine ; we will drink it in mugs,
as one does at the wholesale dealers at Bercy,
and we will sleep in the cellar. Then, too,
a friend of mine, a Dominican monk, un-
frocked only a day or two ago, is coming to
read me a drama in five acts. You will hear

it ; superb subject ! full of rape and ravish-
ment ! Now you understand. Gérard
de Nerval's vineyard ; don't forget the
address !"

All came to pass exactly as Desroches had
promised. We drank out of the cask the
new wine, and in the evening the pretended

Dominican read us his drama. Dominican
or not, he was a fine handsome Breton, with
large shoulders, well fitted for the frock, and
with something of the preacher in the rounding
of his sentences and gestures. He has since
made himself a **name** in literature. **His
drama did not much astonish me, but it must**
be owned **that,** after an afternoon **spent in**
Gérard de Nerval's vineyard—in **what**
Desroches called his home—astonishment
was no longer easy to attain.

Before climbing the slopes **I** had bethought
me **of** re-reading the exquisite pages that
Gérard, the **lover of** *Sylvie*, in his *Promenades
et Souvenirs*, has consecrated to the description of this northern declivity of Montmartre,
a scrap of country inclosed **in the midst of
Paris, and** therefore so **much** the more
cherished and precious : "There still remain
to us a certain number of gently sloping hill-
sides, girdled with thick green hedges, which
the barberry **decorates** alternately with its
violet flowers **and purple berries.** There are
there windmills, **rustic** inns and summer-
houses, elysian fields and deep-cut silent lanes ;
there may even be found **a** vineyard, the last

of the celebrated vintage of Montmartre,
which in the time of the Romans rivalled
those of Argenteuil and Suresnes. Year by
year this humble hillside loses a row of its
stunted vine-stocks, swallowed up by the
stone quarry. Ten years ago I could have
bought it for four hundred pounds. I should
have built in this vineyard so dainty an
edifice ! a little villa in the
Pompeiian style, with an
impluvium and a *cella*."

In this poet's dream of
antiquity lived my friend
Desroches. There ! horrible
antithesis ! did he present
to me, under a blue summer
sky, in the shade of an
arbour of flowering elder,
all musical with the hum of bees, an andlor-
gynous monster in the dress of a carter, blue
smock, short velveteen skirt, cap striped with
red perched over the ear, a whip drawn round
her neck :

" M. Alphonse Daudet, Mme. Desroches!"

For this monster was really his wife, his
legitimate wife, always arrayed in this costume,

which pleased her fancy, and than which,
certainly, nothing could have been found to
suit better with her masculine voice and face.
Smoking, spitting, swearing, with all the vices

of a man, she kept the whole household in
awe ; her husband in the first place, who was
much henpecked, and, besides, two thin
daughters—her daughters !—of strange and
boylike aspect, and who, too early matured

and run to seed, promised at thirteen and
fifteen to become some day all that their
mother was at forty. It certainly was worth
the trouble, as he had said, to have a sight of
such a household.

Desroches was nevertheless the son of a
rich and orderly Parisian manufacturer; a
jeweller, I believe. His father had disowned
him more than once, and now made him a
small allowance. It is not rare to find in
France instances of these lunatics, positive
scourges of Heaven, appearing suddenly in
the midst of peaceful families, troubling their
calm repose, putting in circulation their
accumulated gold, smiting the *bourgeosie* in
short, in its tenderest spot. And I have
known several of these ducklings set under
hens, which, when once out of the shell, rush
to the water. The water, to them, is art,
literature, that trade open to all, without
patent or diploma. Desroches, when he left
college, had dabbled in art—in all the arts.
He had begun with painting, and the career
through the studios of this cool, orderly and
reserved cynic, who preserved in the midst of
the wildest fancies, the indelible stigma of

his *bourgeois* origin, has become a standing
legend.   The attempt at painting proving a
failure, **Desroches** attacked literature.   Inspired perhaps by his vineyard, he managed
to accomplish the *Raisins muscats*—a hundred
lines—a complete article ! Vainly afterwards,
did he try to write another ; he could never
again find the right inspiration, and reached
the age of forty, having as the work of a life-
time, written the *Raisins muscats*.

The conversation and sallies of friend
Desroches amused me ; but his household
did not suit me at all.   I never returned to
Montmartre, but I crossed the river sometimes in order to visit him at the tavern in the
rue des Martyrs. The Brasserie (tavern) of les
Martyrs, nowadays the quiet resort of the
worthy linendrapers of the neighbourhood
for their evening game of draughts, represented then a power in literature.   The
Brasserie sat in judgment ; and made famous
whom it would ; and in the overpowering
silence of the Empire, Paris was aroused by
the noise made there every evening, by eighty
or a hundred choice spirits, while smoking
their pipes and drinking their beer.   They

were called Bohemians, and the name did not displease them. The *Figaro* of that day, non-political, and appearing only once a week, was generally their rostrum.

The tavern was a sight worth seeing—we used to call it "THE BRASSERIE," simply, as the Romans spoke of Rome as "THE CITY,"—it was worth seeing about eleven o'clock at night, with all its cheerful hubbub of voices, and clouded by the smoke of all those pipes!

Murger reigned absolute, at the middle table; Murger, who was at once the Homer and Columbus of this little world, and to which his exquisite fancy lent a rose-coloured tinge. Decorated with the Legion of Honour, and henceforth famous, publishing his stories in the *Revue des deux Mondes*, he nevertheless continued to frequent *the Brasserie*, "to keep alive," he said, "his impressions of the worthy folk he had described, and also to receive their homage and applause." He was pointed out to me—a large, melancholy head, the

eyes reddened, the beard scanty, sure signs
of very indifferent Parisian blood.   He lived
at Marlotte, in the forest of Fontainebleau ;
constantly to be seen with a gun on his shoulder, he pretended to shoot, but it was more a
search after health than after partridges or

hares.   The fact of his abode in the village
had drawn thither quite a Parisian colony of
men and women, natives of the asphalt and
the tavern, producing a strange contrast under the great oaks ; there are traces of it
in Marlotte to this day.   Ten years after the
death of Murger, who died, as all know, in

the Hospital Dubois—I was there with some friends at the famous inn kept by Mother Antony.   An old peasant sat drinking near us, such a peasant as Balzac describes, soil-stained and weatherbeaten.   An old hag, arrayed in tatters, and a red handkerchief round her head, came to fetch him away. She called him drunkard, spendthrift, good-for-nothing ; while he tried to make her drink with him.

"Your wife is none too gentle!" said some one when she was gone.

"She is not my wife ; she is my mistress !" replied the old peasant.

You should have heard the tone in which this was uttered.   Evidently the good man had known Murger and his friends, and sought to lead a Bohemian life according to his lights.

To return to the Brasserie.   As my eyes became accustomed to the smarting caused by the smoke, I could see to the right and left, and in every corner, well-known faces.

Each great man had his table, which became the nucleus, the centre of a whole clique of admirers.

Pierre Dupont, old already at forty-five,

fat and stooping, his mild bovine eye scarcely
visible beneath the drooping eyelids, sat,
elbows on table, trying to sing some of the
political or rustic songs with swinging rhythm,
vibrating still with the fair dreams of '48 ; or
re-echoing the many sounds of work and
labour of the Croix-Rousse, and scented with
the thousand perfumes of the Lyonnaise
valley.   But there was no longer any voice ;
burnt away by alcohol, it was but a hoarse
rattle.

"You require the fresh air of the fields,
my poor Pierre," said Gustave Mathieu, the
bard of *les Bons Vins*, of *le Coq Gaulois*, and of
les Hirondelles.   This last, who came of good
bourgeois blood in Nevers, had travelled
much in his younger days, and retained from
his travels, a passion for fresh air and wide
horizons.   He found all this round his little
house at Bois-le-Roi, and when he came to
the Brasserie, it was only to walk through it
smiling, erect, with a Henri IV. air, and at
all times of the year with a wild flower in
his button-hole.

Dupont died sadly enough in the black
manufacturing town of Lyons.   Mathieu,

tough and healthy as a vine-stock, long
survived him. It is only a few years ago,
that after a short illness his friends laid him
to rest in the little cemetery of Bois-le-Roi—
a cemetery only separated by a simple hedge
from the neighbouring fields—a true poet's

resting-place, where he sleeps beneath roses
in the shadow of the oak-trees.

The evening on which I first saw Gustave
Mathieu, there sat near him a great spare red-
headed fellow with the braggart airs of a
corsair, who imitated his voice and copied
his movements; this was Fernand Desnoyers,

an original, who wrote *Bras-Noir*, a pantomime in verse ! On the other side of the
table some one was arguing with Dupont ; it

was Reyer, who, nervous and excitable, jotted
down the airs which occurred with so much
facility to the poet—Reyer, the future author of
la Statue, of *Sigurd*, and many other fine works.

What memories rise before me at the mere sound of the name of the Brasserie! How many faces did I there behold for the first time amidst the reflections and gleams of the beer-glasses and the canopy of thick smoke!

Let us choose at hazard among the numbers of the departed and the lesser band which yet survives. Here is Monselet, delicate prose writer, yet more dainty poet, smiling, curled, plump. M. Cupid might be taken for a gallant abbé of the olden time; one looks at his back for the short mantle fluttering like a pair of wings. Champfleury, then leader of a school, father of realism, and confounding in one and the same passion the music of Wagner, old pottery, and pantomime. Pottery, in the end, won the day, and Champfleury, transported to the height of his ambition, is now curator of the ceramic museum at Sèvres.

Here too is Castagnary in double-breasted waistcoat, *à la Robespierre*, cut out of the velvet of some old armchair. Chief clerk in a lawyer's office, he used to escape from his work to come and recite the *Châtiments* of Victor Hugo, with all their delightful flavour

of forbidden fruit. He is surrounded, applauded ; but he rushes away in search of
Courbet, he must see Courbet, he wishes to
consult with Courbet upon his *Philosophy of
Art exemplified in the* Salon *of* 1857. Without altogether neglecting art, and while still
contributing with lively pen more than one
remarkable page to our annual Salon, the
shrewd native of Saintonge, always smiling
a mocking smile beneath his long drooping
moustache, has little by little become absorbed in politics. He was first a municipal
councillor, then editor of the *Siècle,* now a
member of the Council of State, and no
longer recites verses nor wears a red velvet
waistcoat.

Here also is Charles Baudelaire, tormented
in art by a thirst for the undiscoverable, in
philosophy by the alluring terror of the unknown. Victor Hugo said of him that he had
invented a perfectly new shudder ; and indeed
by no one has the heart of humanity been
so well persuaded to speak aloud its secrets ;
no one has searched more deeply for those
flowers of evil, startling and strange as
tropical blossoms, with poison lurking in

their very core, which lie in the mysterious
depths of the human soul. Patient and
delicate artist, weighing carefully the turn
of every phrase, the choice of every word,
Baudelaire, by a cruel irony of fate, died
paralyzed, his intelligence remaining intact,
as the mute complaint of his black eye
sorrowfully testified, but incapable of expressing his thoughts save by a confusedly
murmured oath mechanically repeated. Correct and cold, of paradoxical politeness, his
wit as keen as English steel, he astonished
the frequenters of the Brasserie by drinking
foreign liqueurs in company with Constantin
Guys the designer, or Malassis the publisher.

This last was a publisher of a kind unknown nowadays. Witty and well-read in
curious by-ways of literature, he squandered
royally a fine provincial fortune in publishing
the writings of men who pleased his fancy.
He too is dead; died smiling, with scanty
fortune left, but without a complaint. And
it is not without emotion that I recall that
pale mocking face, lengthened by the points
of a red beard—a Mephistopheles of the
time of the Valois.

Alphonse Duchesne and Delvau appear
also in a corner of the tavern—two more
who have joined the majority. It was a
singular fate which pursued this generation,
so early laid low, not one having passed the
age of forty! Delvau, a Parisian, connoisseur
of his Paris, admiring its beauties, loving its
defects, offspring of Mercier and of Rétif de
la Bretonne, whose choice little volumes, full
of small insignificant facts and picturesque
observations, have become the delight of the
literary epicure and the joy of the bibliophile.
Alphonse Duchesne still hot over his great
quarrel with Francisque Sarcey, who, opposing
the standard of the Normal School to that
of the Bohemians, had just launched forth
into literature with a warlike article entitled
Les Mélancoliques de Brasserie (the melancholy
haunters of the tavern).

It was at the Brasserie that Alphonse
Duchesne and Delvau wrote those " Junius'
Letters" which were brought every week to
the *Figaro* by a mysterious messenger, and
which convulsed the whole of Paris. Villemessant swore by that mysterious Junius.
He was clearly a great personage—every·

thing pointed to it—the style of the letters,
their curt yet well-bred tone, a faint perfume
of nobility and the old faubourg clinging
tenderly to them. What then was his rage

when the mask was dropped, and he learned
that these aristocratic pages were written day
by day by two needy Bohemians at a beer-
shop table ! Poor Delvau ! poor Duchesne !
Villemessant never forgave them

I leave out many, for it would take a whole volume to describe the frequenters of the Brasserie table by table. Here is the table of the thinkers; they say nothing, neither do they write; they only think. They are ad-

mired on the faith of their own word; it is said they are deep as a well. It is possible to believe this when one watches them filling themselves with beer. Bald heads, flowing beards, with an odour of strong tobacco, cabbage soup, and philosophy.

A little further on are pilot coats, Spanish birettas, cries of animals, rough jokes, puns, in a glorious confusion ; there crowded together are artists, sculptors, painters.   In the midst of all this appears a refined and gentle head—that of Alexandre Leclerc—whose fantastic frescoes, destroyed by the Prussians, once adorned the walls of the Moulin-de-Pierre inn at Châtillon.

One day the poor fellow was discovered hanged ; he had strangled himself sitting down, and pulling the rope tight, among a crowd of tombstones at the top of the cemetery of Père-Lachaise, just at the spot where Balzac points out the immensity of Paris to Rastignac.   In my recollections of the Brasserie, Alexandre Leclerc always appears in the best of spirits, singing songs of Picardy ; and these rural airs, airs of his native province, seemed to spread around his table in the tobacco-laden atmosphere, a penetrating and poetical aroma of cornfields and green plains.

I had nearly forgotten the women, for there were women too ; former models, fine creatures, but somewhat faded in appearance. Queer physiognomies and strange names,

nicknames that spoke of low haunts and
aristocratic affectations : *Titine de Barancy*
and *Louise Coup-de-Couteau.* Curious speci-
mens of a singular refinement, having passed
from hand to hand, and caught from their
thousand **and one** *liaisons* a veneer of artistic
erudition. They express their opinions **on**
every subject, and according **to the lover of**
the moment, declare themselves materialists
or idealists, catholics or atheists. Touching,
and at the same time somewhat ridiculous.

Amongst them were **a** few new recruits,
quite young, admitted by the dreaded areo-
pagus ; but the majority were composed **of**
those who had grown old in the service,
thereby acquiring a kind of undisputed
authority. Then there were the pseudo-
widows of well-known authors and artists,
who were busily engaged in educating some
raw provincial fellow just arrived from **his**
province. All these people were rolling and
smoking cigarettes, sending up their little
spiral clouds of thin blue smoke amongst the
thick gray fog of the pipes and breaths.

The beer flows, the waiters rush about, the
discussions become more animated, and in

the midst of the shouting and upraised arms, the tossing of many shaggy and mane-like locks, Desroches screaming louder, gesticulating more violently than any, stands on a table, looking as if he were swimming over an ocean of heads, leading and dominating with his clown's voice, the noisy uproar of the thronged room. He looks well thus, with an inspired air, his shirt unbuttoned, his cravat floating half untied, true descendant of Rameau's nephew.

Every night he comes there to forget his worries, to intoxicate himself with words and beer, to secure collaborators, to relate his literary projects, to lie to himself, and to forget that his home has become unbearable, that he is incapable of settling to any work, that it would even be impossible for him to re-write the *Raisins muscats*. No doubt amongst the medley at the tavern there were some noble minds, some serious thinkers, and at times a fine verse or an eloquent paradox would lighten the atmosphere, like a current of fresh, pure air, dispelling the smoke of the pipes. But with the exception of a few men of talent, were not most of

K

them Desroches! For a few moments of
fine inspiration how many dull and wasted
hours!

Then also what a sad feeling the next day.
What cruel awakenings! what sickening dis-
couragement! What disgust for such a life,
without having courage enough to change it.
Look at Desroches; he no longer laughs;
his grin subsides. He is thinking of his
children, who are growing up; of his wife,
who is ageing and sinking lower and lower,
with her whip, her cap, her smock, her
carter's costume, thought so original the first
time it was worn for a masqued ball, and
now become so repulsive.

When his fits of depression were upon him,
Desroches used to disappear and go off into
the provinces, dragging his strange family
after him.

Now selling watches; then actor at Odessa,
bailiff at Brussels; or companion of a mountebank. What extraordinary callings had he
not tried? But he soon returned, tired and
disgusted even with that.

One day, in the Bois de Boulogne, he tried
to hang himself, but the keepers found him

and took him down. He was even chaffed about it at the *brasserie*, and himself spoke of his adventure with a little forced laugh. Shortly after, determined to put an end to his life, he threw himself into one of those terrible quarries—an abyss of chalk and clay —which abound round the Paris fortifications. There he lay all night, his ribs crushed, his wrists and thighs broken. He was still alive when he was taken out.

"Ah, well!" he said, "they will call me the man who always misses his mark."

These were his last words. After an agony which lasted sixty days, he died. I shall never forget him.

THE STORY OF MY BOOKS.

JACK.

In front of me, upon the table, stands a photograph by Nadar, representing a young lad of eighteen or twenty years of age. A delicate, sickly-looking face, with vague and dreamy features, clear, playful and child-like eyes, strangely contrasting, by their vivacity, with the sadness of the weak and faded mouth and its drawn look—the mouth of a poor man, who has suffered much. It is the portrait of Raoul D——, the "Jack" of my

novel, just as I **knew** him towards the end
of 1868 ; just as I used to see him coming
towards the little house **I inhabited** at
Champrosay, shivering, bent, with rounded
shoulders, his arms clasping **tightly his scanty**
wrap across his narrow chest, and coughing
with a sound that echoed like a death knell.
We were **neighbours, separated only by the**
woods of Sénart. Already ill, crushed by
the horrible factory life, to which a caprice
of his mother's lover had condemned him,
he had come in search **of rest** and quiet to
a large lonely building in the country, where
he led a kind of Robinson Crusoe existence,
with a sack of potatoes, and **a running account**
for bread at **the Soisy baker's shop. He had**
no money, not even enough to take the train
to Paris ; and **when** the longing to see his
mother became too unbearable, **he** trudged
the eighteen tedious miles on foot, and came
back, worn out and exhausted, but thoroughly
happy ; for he adored his mother, speaking
of her **with** a tender, admiring effusiveness,
something like the respect that the half-breed
feels for the white **woman, for** the superior
being. " Mamma is a canoness," he said **to**

me one day, with so satisfied an air that I
did not dare to ask him of what chapter.
Nevertheless, several things he had said,
made me understand the character of this
misguided woman, who, notwithstanding her
love of rank and her aristocratic pretensions,
had consented to make a mere mechanic of
her son.   Did she not tell him on one occasion that he was the son of the Marquis de
P——, a well-known name under the Empire?
And the notion of being the son of a noble-
man amused the poor fellow, and threw a
glimmer of vanity over his sad and miserable
life and low coffee-house fare.   Later on,
forgetting her first avowal, she told him his
father was an artillery officer, without its being
possible to guess on which occasion she had
lied, or if she spoke truthfully, at the haphazard of her capricious vanity and over-
crowded recollections.   In my book, this
characteristic detail has shocked many of
my readers; drawn from the very life, it
seemed an exaggeration of the psychologist,
who, however, would have shrunk from such
an invention.

Well, even this, Raoul forgave his mother,

and he never showed any greater trace of
bitterness than a sad, deprecating smile,
which seemed to ask pardon for the irre-
sponsible offender. " It cannot be helped ;
it is just like her." It must not be forgotten, however, that the lower class is devoid
of much refinement and delicacy in its ideas
of morality, and Raoul formed part of that
class, among whom he had been thrown from
the early age of eleven, after a few short
months spent in a fashionable school at
Auteuil. Of this attempt at education he
had retained only a few vague notions, names
of authors, titles of books, and a love of
study which he had never been able to
satisfy. Now however, when all physical
exertion had been strictly forbidden him by
the doctor, and that my library shelves were
thrown open to him, he revelled in them,
seizing upon the books with the avidity of
a hungered man. He would go off laden
with books for his evenings and for his
nights—those long weary nights of fever and
cough, which he spent in his dimly-lighted
house, shivering in his miserable bed, even
though he had heaped upon it the whole of

his wretched wardrobe. But above all, he enjoyed **reading** in my house, seated in the **window recess of the room** I worked in, **looking out on the fields** and the Seine.

"**Here I seem** to understand better," he **would say.** Sometimes I helped him to understand; **for, moved by a** kind of superstitious feeling, an ambitious turn of mind, **he always** chose difficult authors—Montaigne, La **Bruyère.** "One of Balzac's or Dickens's novels amused him too much," he **said, and failed** to give him the proud satisfaction of **conquering a** difficulty, which the **laborious perusal of classical** work afforded **him.** In the pauses of rest I made him talk **to me of his life and of the** working class, **which he intuitively judged** with a keenness **of observation far beyond** his age and position. **He felt** the painful as well as the **ridiculous** side of things, and the grandeur **of** certain aspects of factory life. For instance, the starting of the machine **I** describe in *Jack* is one of his 'prentice recollections. **But what I found most** interesting **was the awakening and** refining of **this** mind, which revived like a dormant memory under

the exciting influence of the **books and our**
conversations. A change was even taking
place in the physical being raised up by the
intellectual effort. **Unfortunately the exi-**
gencies of life were **about to separate us ;**
and while **I** returned to Paris **for the** winter,
Raoul taking up his workman's tools, engaged
himself in the workshops of the Lyons **rail-**
way company. During the following **six**
months, I only saw him two or three times **;**
each time thinner and more altered, and **in**
a state **of** utter despair, feeling **that he was**
decidedly too weak for his work. "**Well,**
leave it, we will find you another." **But** he
insisted upon struggling **on,** lest he should
grieve his mother; feeling himself **wounded**
in the **pride of** his manhood. **Not aware**
that he **was in** so dangerous **a condition,**
I dared not insist, fearing above all things
lest I should make him dissatisfied **with** his
lot, and take this poor artisan with a romantic
name, out of his proper sphere.

Time went by. One day I received a **few**
shaky and piteous lines : " Ill ; laid up at the
hospital *de la Charité*, ward *St. Jean de Dieu*."
It was there I found him again, lying on a

stretcher ; the winter, which was drawing to
an end, having been so severe that there was
not a vacant bed in the ward devoted to the
consumptive patients. The first bed left
vacant by death would be given to Raoul.
He seemed to me very seriously ill ; the eyes
sunken, the voice hoarse, the imagination
cruelly affected by the prevailing sadness, the
moans, the harrowing coughs, the sister of
mercy's prayer at nightfall, and the chaplain,
who in red slippers brought his ministering
comfort to the agonies of the dying. He
was terrified at the idea of dying there. I
tried to reassure him, although I could not
help expressing my surprise that his mother
did not bring him home to nurse. "It was
I who refused," replied the unhappy victim ;
"they were adding to their house, building—
I should have been in the way." Then,
answering the silent reproach he saw in my
eyes, he added, "Oh, mamma is very kind ;
she writes to me and comes to see me." I
am convinced that he lied ; his miserable
condition, the bareness of his hospital cover-
let, the absence of any little delicacy, not
even an orange, spoke of his abandoned and

neglected state. Seeing him so lonely, so
unhappy, I conceived the idea of making
him write down what he saw around him,
what he too was undergoing, convinced that
his mind would thereby take a higher view
of his surroundings. And then who knows?
it might become a pecuniary aid to the proud
fellow who could with difficulty be induced
to accept a gift of money. At the first
suggestion, the invalid raised himself up,
clinging with both hands to the wooden
handles hanging over the head of his bed.

"Really, is it really true—do you think I
could write?"

"I am certain of it."

As it turned out, I had hardly to change
ten words in the four articles Raoul sent me
from the hospital. Their tone was simple
and sincere, and of an intense realism well
suited to their title "Life in a Hospital."
Those who may have read these short pages
in an ephemeral medical review, the *Journal
d'Enghien*, will assuredly never have supposed that they were written from a hospital
bed with such efforts and at the cost of such
feverish heat. He was so happy too when

I brought him the few gold pieces earned
by his prose ! He could hardly believe it,
turning them over and over again, while in
the beds near him, faces full of curiosity
leaned forward at the unusual sound. From
that day forth, the hospital presented a less
dreary aspect to him, cheered by the study
he was making of it. A short time after,
thanks to a spontaneous effort of youth, he
was able to leave ; but the house-surgeon did
not conceal from me the dangerous state he
was in. The injury to the lung still remained
incurable, ready to break forth afresh at any
moment, whenever the unfortunate fellow
should resume his hard mechanic's life. I
then remembered that when I was the same
age, and in a critical state of health, a few
months spent in Algeria had been of the
greatest benefit to me. I wrote to the
prefect of Algiers, with whom I had a slight
acquaintance, asking him for some employment for Raoul. No doubt M. Le Myre de
Vilers, now the representative of France at
Madagascar, does not remember this, but I
have not forgotten with what alacrity and
good nature—thereby doubly enhancing the

kindliness—he answered my request, offering
Raoul a situation in the official surveyor's
office ; five hours' work per diem, work without fatigue in the most lovely country in the
world, in the midst of fresh green scenery and
with the blue sea spread out before his eyes.

For Raoul this departure seemed quite
like a fairy tale—the long journey, the
happy thought that he would never return
to the factory, that he would no longer have
dirty black hands, and that he would be able
to gain his daily bread without killing himself
by such cruel and uncongenial work. In my
family circle I am surrounded by kind beings
with large and noble hearts, who had been
touched by this unfortunate lad's sufferings,
and they vied with each other in contributing
to his comfort. "I will pay the journey,"
said our good grandmamma ; another took
charge of his linen, another of his clothes,
for he must throw aside the blue jersey and
dirty working-suit of the factory. Raoul
accepted everything now that he had a
situation, and the certainty of being able to
refund all expenses. Only fancy, sixty pounds
a year ! Besides, he would write ; he would

send me articles. He planned many other schemes of happiness, which he discussed with me on the eve of his departure : his mother must come to him, and with him take up the thread again of a more happy and dignified life. She had lived long enough with others; it was his turn now. Looking well in his new clothes, his eyes bright, his face once again handsome and intelligent as he stood speaking to me, he no longer seemed the wretched forlorn creature I had known formerly, but my companion, one of my own belongings, who was taking leave of me, and whom I was never to behold again.

He often wrote to me from Algiers, "I dream! I dream! It seems to me that I am in heaven!" He lived in one of the suburbs, separated from the sea by an orange-grove, near one of my friends, a painter, to whom I had recommended him, as well as to Charles Jourdan, who readily opened his large and hospitable house of Montriant to the poor exile. His office work was light, and gave him ample leisure to continue his education, following the programme of read-

ing I had traced out for him. But it was
already too late when we rescued him from
his misery. He had suffered so terribly, and
so . young ! the wounds of childhood had
deepened with manhood. "I have been
very ill," Raoul wrote to me in a letter dated
18th June, 1870, "but thanks to an energetic
treatment, I am up again, weak, very weak,
it is true, and counting every step I take.
During the fortnight of my convalescence,
while I was unable to move out, my imagination took many a stroll with you through
the forest, and we had many a talk in the
large studio. My head was too weak to
allow of my reading, and I was rather lonely
and sad, immersed in day dreams, when the
kind giant, Charles Jourdan, came to fetch
me with a donkey, and carried me off to
a house, which would be the dearest in the
world to me, if Champrosay did not exist.
At Montriant, the air is so pure, the view so
lovely, the silence so deep, that I feel I am
returning again to life. What a delightful
fellow Jourdan is ! so full of heart and youth !
His study is a regular library, and I spend
my days turning over the pages right and

left, as I used to do at your house.   He
dictates to me his articles for the *Siècle*
and *l'Histoire.*   This morning we cut up the
local administration in merciless style. . . ."
The tone of his letter was cheerful, but one
could feel a real fatigue running through it
all ; and towards the end the tall straight
handwriting became sloping, the ink changed
in colour ; he had evidently been obliged to
interrupt his letter and to complete it by
degrees.

Then the war broke out, the siege followed.   I heard no more about Raoul, and
I forgot him.   Which of us during those long
five months thought of anything else but our
unhappy country ?   Directly Paris was set
free, amongst the piles of letters which
covered my table, I found one from an
Algerian doctor informing me that Raoul
was very ill, and begged for some news of
his mother ; it would be an act of charity if
I could send any.   Why did the mother, who
had likewise been warned, give no sign of
life to her child ?   I have never known why.
But on the 9th of February she received
the following indignant lines from Charles

Jourdan: "Madame, your son is at the hospital; he is dying. He asks for news of his mother. In the name of mercy send two words in your own handwriting to the child you will see no more!"

Shortly after the following news reached me :—

"Raoul died at the civilian hospital of Algiers on the 13th of February, after a long and painful agony. To the very last, he craved for the kiss his mother denied him. 'I suffer dreadfully,' he said to me, 'but I feel that one word from my mother would ease my pain.' That word never came, was never sent. . . . Believe me, that woman has been cruel and pitiless to her child. Raoul adored his mother; nevertheless, on his death bed he judged her with terrible severity. 'I can neither esteem her as a mother, nor as a woman; but my heart, which will so soon cease to beat, is full of her. I forgive her all the harm she has done me.' Raoul spoke about you a great deal before his death. In the midst of his sad life of suffering he was astonished at finding one tender and sweet recollection. 'Tell

him that, at the moment of quitting this life,
it is he and his dear wife whom I regret to
lose.' I had become very intimate with the
poor invalid you had sent us. I inhabit a
large country place full of sunshine and
flowers. I wished Raoul to come and go
as he liked, but the gentle and excellent
young man was always afraid of intruding.
In these latter days, I begged him to come
and be nursed at my house. He refused,
and went to the hospital, pretending he
would be better taken care of there. In
reality the poor child felt his end approaching, and would not distress a friend with the
sad sight of his death. . . .'

* *

This is what real life brought before me.
For a long time I only saw in this story one
of the many thousand sorrows that cross our
own sorrows. It had all taken place too
near to me to attract my attention as a
novelist. The study was hidden from me
by personal emotion. One day at Champrosay, seated on the trunk of a tree by the
side of Gustave Droz, in the autumn melancholy of the woods, within a few paces of the

red brick building where so many of Raoul's
hours of forlorn illness had been spent, I
related to him the story of that miserable
existence.

"What a fine book it would make!" Droz
remarked, much moved.

From that day, putting aside the *Nabab*,
which was then in process of construction, I
started on this new track with the feverish
haste, the tremblingly eager fingers, with
which I begin and end all my books. In
comparing the story of Raoul with that of
Jack, it is easy to distinguish what is real
from what is imaginary, or, at least—for I
invent but little—what I have introduced
from other sources. Raoul never lived at
Indret, and he was never a stoker. Nevertheless he has often related to me how, at
Havre, during his apprenticeship, the air,
full of the sounds of travel—vibrating with
the cries of the sailors, the blows of the
hammers in the graving dock—sometimes
filled him also with the longing to be afloat,
and to accompany in its voyage round the
world, one of those gigantic engines turned
out by the house of Mazeline.

The whole episode of Indret is imaginary. I wanted a great iron-manufacturing centre, and I hesitated between Creuzot and Indret. I decided in favour of the latter, on account of the river life, the scenes on the Loire and the port of Saint Nazaire. This gave occasion for a journey and for many expeditions during the summer of 1874. Having placed my little Jack there, I wished to know in what surroundings, among what human entities, I must make him live. I have spent many an hour in the isle of Indret, and haunted the vast workshops both during the working hours and in those, so much richer in impressions, of rest. I have seen the house of the Roudics with its little garden; I have gone up and down the Loire from Saint Nazaire, in a crazy boat which rolled as much and seemed as drunk as its old boatman, who was greatly astonished that I did not rather take the rail at Basse Indre, or the steamboat at Paimbœuf; and the wharf, the transatlantic steamers, the engine rooms, visited in detail, furnished me with closely kept notes for my study.

On these excursions, I was nearly always

accompanied by my wife and my little boy—I
had only one at that time—a dear little pickle

with ruddy curls, who displayed at these
amazingly novel scenes, his simple and

childish surprise. When the expedition
promised to be too rough, the mother and
child awaited me in a little inn at Piriac,
a real Breton inn, white and square as a die,
on the edge of the great ocean; it owned a
huge bedroom with rustic beds; one of them
let into the whitewashed wall, cupboard
fashion; the chimney piece was adorned
with sponges and sea-horses, as at the
Roudics; and two little windows fastened
by that transverse bar common to the coast,
overlooked, one the pier and the vast expanse
of sea, while from the other could be seen
orchards, a bit of the church, and the
cemetery full of black crosses, crowding
and jostling each other, as if the rolling
of the neighbouring waves, and the wind
from the open sea, shook even the tombs of
the sea-faring population. Beneath us, a
thought noisy on a Sunday evening, was the
tap-room, where one could hear sung the old
airs of the district, which re-live again in my
book. Sometimes, when the great brigadier
Mangin was there—he really was the brigadier
Mangin, for I have not even changed his name
or rank—our host would allow the benches

to be pushed back, and a dance to take place, "with a singing accompaniment." Thither came with their wives, the fishermen and sailors, who had become friendly with us, taking us in their boats to breakfast on the island of Dumet, or even to some rock out at sea. They knew that a little swell frightened neither my little Parisian nor his mother; and one of them, an old whaler, once said to us, that, when he looked at Monsieur, Madame and the little boy, always travelling together, it reminded him, begging our pardon, of three North Sea blowers which always moved in company: father, mother, and young whale.

In all our excursions there was no question of anything but Jack. We seemed to live so entirely with him, that to-day, in thinking of this corner of Brittany, I imagine my poor Raoul must have been of the party. When we returned to Paris, I did not set to work at once. There was still wanting to my work, notes on the life of the Parisian work-girl. I only knew of it all that may be learned in the street, of its misery, debauches, struggles; but what of the factory, the wine shop, the tea gardens on the banks of the lake of *Saint-Mandé*, where I have represented the wedding of Belisarius; the dust of *les Buttes-Chaumont*, where I have dawdled away many a Sunday afternoon, drinking sour beer and watching the kite flying? As for the hospital which holds so large and so mournful a place in the life of the lower class, I knew it well.

I had spent long hours there, during Raoul's illness, and had also derived much information from his articles. But as the Goncourt brothers had described the hospital of *La Charité* once and for all in *Sœur Philomène*, I could not, and after them, begin again upon the same subject. Therefore, I barely touched upon it, and only in very brief passages. In the third part of *Jack*, the recollections were those of the siege, the National Guard, which were of the greatest service to me, and the workmen's battalion, with which I scoured Paris and the outskirts during four months, sleeping in the damp wooden sheds, or on the straw of cattle trucks; and in these experiences, learning to love the people even in their vices, caused as they are by misery and ignorance. The

Belisarius of my book—Offehmer was his
real name—was with me in the *sixth* of the
ninety-sixth, and I can see him yet, with his
huge and deformed feet, breaking the line
by his limp, always the last of the company
in the interminable rue de Charenton. Denis
Poulot's book, *Le Sublime*, to which Zola's
fine novel has since given popularity, was also
of great help to me, filled as it is with typical
expressions and the special slang pertaining
to certain trades, just as I also found in the
Manuel Roret and the *Grandes Usines* of Tur-
gan, many technical details of the working life
of these great factories which were new to me.
This then, is the foundation of a novel; the
preparation, slow as possible and full and
close, from which must spring for the
writer, the invention, the style, the real merit
of the work. And to think that there are people
who, two months after a new publication, ask :
" When will your next book appear ? Come !
get on, lazy bones."

The failures and their surroundings cost
me much less trouble and research. I had
only to look behind me in my five and twenty
years' experience of Paris. The high priest

Dargenton existed, just as I have drawn him,
with his forehead out of all proportion, his
imaginary fits, his blind and fierce egoism of
an impotent Buddha. Not one of his "bitter
sayings" is invented. I gathered them fresh,
as they fell from his fruitful lips; his faith in
his own genius was just such as I have
described it at full length in my book;
solemn, black and gloomy as a country
sheriff, he no doubt smiled scornfully on
reading it, and said, "Envy! mere envy!"
Labassindre may be seen ten times over in a
café well known on the boulevards, during
summer, the idle times of such actors.
Hirsch is a more peculiar type: twenty
years ago I used daily to see this would-be
doctor, with a bottle of ammonia peeping out
of the pocket of his vast nankin waistcoat;
dirty, infatuated, bent upon visiting and
drugging whom he could, notwithstanding
his lack of diploma. He had always some
victim in hand, upon whom he was studying
the effect of unusual and dangerous medi-
cines; then, for want of patients, he took
to dosing himself, and died at the hospital of
Bordeaux, in consequence of his own reme-

dies. Moronval, the mulatto, was a living
being too, he wrote in the *Revue Coloniale*,
and after 1870, was for some time a deputy.
He inhabited, when I knew him, a little house
with a garden, at Batignolles, and lived upon
half a dozen little niggers sent over from
Port-au-Prince, or Tahiti, who were at once
pupils and servants, going to market for him,
and blacking boots, while they construed the
Epitome.

Of the real and living drama I have in the
main kept the principal personage, and the
chief outlines of his hard life and sad death.
I did not know the mother, but I have represented her as I guessed her from the narrative
of her child. True to life again, and excellent as truth itself, was the noble Doctor
Rivals, a saint, a hero, who had frequented
for thirty years those roads so familiar to
Jack and his novelist. For fear of annoy-
ing him and of offending his great modesty
I dare not here give his name, which a whole
population of peasants has blessed for two
generations. I trust he will forgive me for
having in the composition of my story worked
into his noble life—so open and upright—a

dark drama drawn from other sources.[1]   I
had nearly forgotten two other witnesses of
Raoul's sad misery, the gamekeeper's wife,
who still inhabits the humble cottage in the
forest, where more than once the poor little
fellow was given a place by the fire and at
the table ; and old Salé, to whom I left her
real name, the old hooked-nosed peasant,
the dread of the poor abandoned child, who
dreamt of her during the long nights in his
hospital-bed.   It is sometimes a weakness
of mine to leave to my models their real
names, and to persuade myself that were the
name transformed, it would take away something from the integrity of the creation, which
is nearly always a reminiscence of real life,
of haunting, wearying phantoms, only laid
when I fix them in my work as life-like as
possible.

⁎

All this foundation well established, my
figures on the scene, my chapters arranged
in their place, I set to work.   My workshop

[1] He is dead now, his name was Doctor Rouffy;
his bust adorns the pretty village green at Draveil.

was still the large study with two high and
wide windows in the Palace Lamoignon.
In the first pages of the chapter entitled
Jack en ménage, you may see the horizon of
artisan dwellings, of zinc roofs, of tall factory
chimneys bound round with iron cordage,
which through the streaming panes and the
fog of Parisian daylight, greeted my view
whenever I raised my eyes from the paper. In
the evening, all the windows crowded together
in these tall frontages were lighted on every
floor, revealing shadows of brave toilers,
figures bending over their work far into the
night, especially towards New Year's Day,
the stalls and booths of which were supplied
chiefly by this colony of toy-sellers. But
the best pages of all were written at Champrosay, where the first blossoming lilac saw
us arrive for a summer residence, often
prolonged till the appearance of the first
snows.

The best guarded, the most carefully
closed of our Paris houses, are yet open to
many unforeseen distractions. It may be
the friend who brings for your sympathy
his joy or his anxiety ; the morning paper

full of stirring news; the shameless bore who
will **not** be denied; and the mill round of
society; dinners, first nights, from which the
observer, the painter of modern manners,
has scarcely the right to absent himself. In
the country, the space is vast, the air fresh,
time seems endless; and free to dispose at
will **of the** long days and of self, one feels
above all, the security of this independence,
the reassuring sensation of being really alone
with one's idea. It is an orgie of thought
and of work. I never felt it more so than
when writing *Jack.* This time of un-
ceasing production has left to me delightful
memories. **Long** before daylight, I was
installed at my white wood table close to
my bed **in** the dressing-room. I wrote by
lamplight, beneath a skylight pearled with
dew, which reminded me of my early years
of poverty. Cats and other roamers of the
night prowled upon the roof, scratching the
tiles, an owl hooted, cattle lowed in the
warm straw of a stable close by; and with-
out glancing at the alarum-clock ticking in
front of me, without lifting my eyes to the
gradual lightening of the dawn, I knew the

hour by the crowing of the cocks, by the
sounds of movement in the neighbouring
farm, whence rose a clatter of wooden shoes,
of bucket-handles falling as the beasts were
watered ; gruff voices hailing each other in
the chill grey of early day, and the clamour,
the cackling and flapping of heavy wings.
Then upon the road, the sleepy tramp of
workpeople passing by in gangs ; and a little
later, a flock of children running to the
school three miles off, sounding like the
passing flight of a covey of partridges.

What excited me and urged me to this
breathless haste of labour, was that, from
the month of June, and long before I had
finished my book, Paul Dalloz had begun the
publication of it in the *Moniteur*. I have the
habit, which may seem in contradiction to my
slow and conscientious method of work, of
handing over in advance to the journals, the
first finished chapters of a book. By this, I
gain the absolute necessity of separating myself from my work, without further yielding
to the tyrannous desire for perfection which
makes an artist correct too much and re-

commence ten, twenty, times the same page.
I **know** some who thus exhaust themselves,
and for years expend their energies without
result, upon the same work ; paralysing their
real qualities and finally producing only
what I may call "literature of the deaf," of
which the beauties and niceties are at length
appreciated only by themselves.

I **gain** also a spur to my natural indolence ;
the *lazzaronisme* of my race that causes me
to detest long-continued efforts of attention
or reflection, and which in me is accompanied
by a horrible faculty for critical analysis.
However, when once in the water, swim one
must, and **that is** why I throw myself into
it resolutely.

But what fears, what terrors ensue ; and
then the dread of falling ill, and the anguish
of feeling that *feuilleton* with giant strides
perpetually treading upon one's heels !

Jack was finished towards the end of
October.   I had taken nearly a year to write
it.   It is much the longest, and also the most
quickly finished of any of my books.   Thus

it was that the completion of it left me in a
state of prostration from which I went to
recover, always accompanied by my two dear
travelling companions, in the glorious sunshine of the Mediterranean coast, among the
violets of Bordighera. There I spent days
of positive mental convalescence, with the
silences, the absorbed contemplation of
nature, the delightful draughts of pure and
reviving air, which follow a severe illness.
On my return *Jack* was published by Dentu,
in two thick volumes, and had not the same
successful sale as *Fromont Jeune*. Two
volumes to our French customs appear both
long and dear. "A little too much paper
about it, my boy," my good Flaubert, to
whom it is dedicated, said to me, with his
kind smile. I was reproached also with
having too much insisted on the sufferings
of the poor martyr. Georges Sand wrote to
me that she rose from reading them with
such a terrible heart-ache that "she remained
three days without having been able to
work." The impression must indeed
have been vivid that could change the

L

course of this courageous and imperturbable worker.

Yes! it is indeed a sad, bitter, cruel tale. But what is it after all compared with the *real existence* which I have just related.

L'ÎLE DES MOINEAUX.

(SPARROW ISLAND.)

A Meeting on the Seine.

AT that time I did not suffer from rheumatism, and for six months of the year I worked in my boat. It was on a lovely bend of the river, about thirty miles above Paris, where the Seine is provincial, countrified, and fresh, where reeds and rushes, iris and water-lily, encroach upon its waters, and tufts of long grass and roots float about, on which the water wagtails, tired by flight, abandon themselves to the course of the stream. On the

slopes of each bank, cornfields, squares of
vineyard ; here and there a few green islands
dotted about ;—l'ile des Paveurs, l'ile des
Moineaux—this last quite small, a mere
nosegay of brambles and straggling branches,
which had become my favourite mooring-
place. I used to push my dingy between
the reeds, and when the soft rustling of the
long slight canes had ceased and my wall was
well closed in around me, I found myself in
a tiny harbour of clearest water, hollowed
under the shade of an old willow which
served me as a study, the two oars crossed
before me making a desk. I loved the smell
of the river, the hum of the insects among
the rushes, the murmur of the long quivering
leaves, all that mysterious, infinite agitation
which the silence of man awakes in nature !
To how vast a multitude this silence brings
happiness ! To what millions of little beings
is it reassuring ! My islet was more popu-
lous than Paris. I heard busy creatures
hunting and ferreting beneath the grass, the
flight of birds pursuing each other through
the branches, the shaking of damp feathers
spread out to dry. No one paid any attention

to me; they took me for an old willow. The black dragon-flies shot by under my nose, the water-flies bespattered me in their luminous leaps, the swallows came to drink actually beneath the oars.

One day, on penetrating into my island, I found my solitude invaded by a yellow beard and a straw hat. That was all I beheld at first,—a yellow beard and a straw hat. The intruder was not fishing; he lay at full length in his boat, his oars crossed like mine. He was working too, working in my study! At first sight both our faces expressed the same feeling of annoyance. Nevertheless we bowed. There was no help for it; the shadow cast by the willow was limited and our two boats touched. As he did not appear inclined to go away I settled myself without saying a word, but this hat with a beard to it so near to me disturbed my train of thought. Probably I too embarrassed him. Inaction made us speak. My boat was called *L'Arlésienne*, and the name of Georges Bizet served at once as a point of contact.

"You know Bizet? Are you by chance

an artist?" The beard smiled and replied modestly,

"Sir, I am in the musical line."

Generally speaking, literary people have a horror of music. Gautier's opinion on "the most disagreeable of all noises" is well known ; Leconte de Lisle and Banville share it. The moment a piano is opened Goncourt frowns. Zola has a vague impression that he once, in his youth, played some instrument, he no longer remembers what it was. That excellent Flaubert pretended to be a great musician, but it was only to please Tourguéneff, who in reality never cared for any music but that heard at the Viardots. As for me I love every kind madly—the classic, the simple, Beethoven, Gluck and Chopin, Massenet and Saint-Saëns, the *bamboula*, the *Faust* of Gounod and that of Berlioz, popular songs, grinding organs, the tambourine and even bells. Music that dances,

music that dreams, all speak to me, all awake
an answering chord within me. The
Wagnerian chant seizes me, envelops me,

hypnotizes me like
the sea; and the
wild strains of the
Tziganes prevented
me from seeing the
Exhibition. Every
time those confounded
violins caught me as I
passed along, it was
impossible to go further.
There I must remain till
evening with a glass of Hungarian wine before
me, a choking in the throat, eyes staring.

and my whole body quivering to the nervous
beat of the dulcimer.

This musician falling upon my islet won
my heart.   His name was Léon Pillaut.
He had wit, ideas, a pretty imagination ; we
suited each other at once.   Started by nearly
the same things, our paradoxes made common
cause.   From this day, my island belonged
to him as much as to me ; and as his boat,
a Norwegian craft without a keel, rolled
horribly, he got into the habit of coming to
talk of music in mine.   His book—*Instruments et Musiciens,* which caused him to be
named Professor at the Conservatoire—was
already running in his head, and he used
to relate it to me.   We lived that book
together.

I read between the lines of it the pleasant
intimacy of our gossip, just as I used to see
the Seine dancing between my reeds.   Pillaut
set forth to me absolutely new views upon
his art.   A talented musician, brought up in
the country, his trained and delicate ear retained and noted all the varied sounds of
nature ; he heard as a landscape-painter sees.
For him every flutter of wings gave its par-

ticular thrill. The confused hum of insects, the dry rattle of autumn leaves, the babbling of the brooks over the pebbles, the wind, the rain, far-off voices, the distant rumble of the train, wheels creaking in the ruts—all this country life and being may be found in his book. And many other things too— ingenious criticisms, a pleasant and erratic erudition, the poetical biography of the orchestra and all instruments, from the amorous viola to the Saxony horn—all related for the first time. We talked of it beneath our willow or in some inn by the riverside, while we drank the muddy white wine of the year's vintage, and split a herring on the edge of a chipped plate in the midst of quarrymen and mariners ; we talked of it as we pulled the oar, exploring the Seine and the unknown streamlets which fall into it.

Oh ! what expeditions we made upon the pretty *Orge,* dappled with light, black with shade, tangled with scented cords of briar and climbers, as a brooklet of the tropics ! We went straight on without knowing whither. Sometimes for a moment we passed between civilized lawns, whereon a white peacock

trailed his tail, and bright-coloured dresses
gleamed like flowers. A picture by Nittis.
In the background, the house, all radiant with
its galaxy of beauty, was shadowed by thick
and lofty foliage, from which trilled forth the
sonorous roulades and cheerful twittering of
those cage birds kept by the rich. Further
on we found again the wild flowers of our
island, the straggling branches, the twisted
and gnarled gray willows; or else some old
windmill, tall as a round tower, with its moss-
grown gallery, great walls with irregular loop-
holes, and on the roof a crowd of pigeons
and guinea fowl, amongst whom was a continual shiver and rustle of wings which
seemed to be put in movement by the heavy
machinery. Then came the return down
stream with the current, singing old ditties!
The screech of the peacock resounded on
the deserted lawns; in the middle of a grass
field stood the little cart of the shepherd,
who was collecting his beasts from a distance
to fold them for the night. We disturbed
the kingfisher, the blue bird of the little
streams; we bent ourselves double at the
mouth of the *Orge* to pass beneath the low

arch of the bridge, and then all at once the Seine opening out before us in the rolling mists, gave us the impression of the open sea.

Amid so many charming wanderings one above all is imprinted on my mind — an autumn breakfast at an inn by the waterside. I see again the chilly morning, the leaden, melancholy Seine, the landscape beautiful in its stillness, while low over the land lay a penetrating mist, which made us turn up the collars of our coats. The inn was a little above the lock at Coudray, an old posting-house, where the inhabitants of Corbeil are wont to spend a joyous Sunday, but which, out of the season, is only frequented by the people who use the lock—crews of the barges and tugs. At that moment the soup was smoking hot, ready for the passing of the gang. What a delicious puff of hot scent greeted us on entering. "And what after the beef, gentlemen? How would a stewed tench suit you?" That tench was exquisite, served up on a coarse earthenware plate in a little parlour, the wall-paper of which had a pleasant air of *bourgeois*

merry-making about it. The meal finished
and pipes lighted, we began to talk of Mozart.
It was truly an autumn conversation. Outside on the little terrace in front of the inn
I could see through the leafless arbours a
swing, painted green, a game of *tonneau*,
the targets of a crossbow shooting-gallery, all
shivering in the teeth of a cold wind off the
Seine, and wearing the air of mournful
sadness peculiar to abandoned pleasure
haunts. "Ah, a spinet!" said my companion, lifting the dusty cover of a long
table covered with plates. He tried the
instrument, drew from it a few cracked
and bleating sounds, and till evening closed
we bemused ourselves delightfully with
Mozart.

FROMONT JEUNE ET RISLER AÎNÉ.

THE first idea of *Fromont Jeune* occurred to me during a grand rehearsal of *l'Arlésienne* at the Vaudeville Theatre. Before a magnificent scene of the Camargue, blazing under jets of gas to the very background, were unfolded the slow and rhythmical scenes of the pastoral, accompanied by ancient carols and antique marches, expressed in the charming music of Bizet. Seated before this impassioned fairy tale, that charmed my Southern

heart, but which I divined to be somewhat too local, too slight in action, I said to
myself that the Parisians would soon tire of
hearing me talk of *cicalas*, of the daughters
of Arles, of the mistral, and of my windmill ;
that it was time to interest them in some
work which should speak of things nearer
to them, to their every-day life in their
own atmosphere ; and as I then lived in the
Marais, I naturally bethought me of placing
my drama in the midst of the energetic
labour of this mercantile quarter.   The
association tempted me : the son of a manufacturer myself, I was well acquainted with
the inner workings of commercial collaboration, where similar interests draw together, for
the business of a day, and sometimes for years,
beings of the most various temperament and
education.   I knew well the jealousies between household and household, the bitter
rivalry of the women, amongst whom castes
exist and struggle far more than amongst men,
and all the petty worries of a roof shared with
others.   At Nismes, Lyons, or Paris,—I had
more models than enough, and all in my own
family, and I began to think of this piece, of

which the pivot of the action must be the mercantile value of the signature and the firm.

Unfortunately, whatever happens, there must be some passion in a play. Adultery, with all its dangers, its emotions, never fails to attract; and thus it is that the interest of my study is lessened and misplaced, being concentrated upon Sidonie and her adventures, when the association should be the principal interest; but I fully intend to return to this subject some day.

L'Arlésienne, as every one knows, was not a success. It was unreasonable to suppose that in the middle of the boulevard, in that coquettish corner of the Chaussée-d'Antin, right in the pathway of the fashions, the whims of the hour, the flashing and changing vortex of all Paris, any one could be interested in this drama of love, taking place in a farmyard in a plain of Camargue, full of the odour of well-plenished granaries and lavender in flower. It was a splendid failure; clothed in the prettiest music possible, with costumes of silk and velvet in the centre of comic-opera scenery. I came away dis-

couraged and sickened, the silly laughter
with which the emotional scenes were greeted
still ringing in my ears; and without attempt-
ing to defend myself in the papers, where on
all sides the attack was led against this play
wanting in surprises, this painting in three
acts, of manners and events of which I alone
could appreciate the absolute fidelity, I re-
solved to write no more plays, and heaped
one upon the other all the hostile notices
as a rampart around my determination.
Fromont, which was devised, thought out,
almost to completion, appeared to me capable of transmutation into a novel. I ought
then to have changed the setting of the
intrigue, re-arranged the order and the gra-
dation of the sentiments; but nothing is
more difficult than to upset a piece of work
where the fragments hold together in close
assemblage and are completely fitted as a
mosaic; nothing is more unwelcome than
the voluntary destruction of conceptions
long nursed in the mind and vivid in their
melancholy. And the elements of the drama
—I mean by this the drama such as I had
imagined it, not as it was afterwards played

—having served me for the groundwork of
the novel, explains how the plot of *Fromont
jeune* is a little conventional and romantic
with types and surroundings strictly copied
from nature.

Copied from nature!

I have never followed any other method.
Just as painters carefully keep their albums
full of sketches where the outlines, attitudes,
foreshortenings and movements of the limbs
are caught on the spur of the moment, so
have I for the last thirty years, collected a
quantity of memoranda, in which I have re-
corded my observations, my passing thoughts,
sometimes jotted down in a few short words
sufficient to recall a picture, an intonation,
which later on I have enlarged upon and
brought into harmony with the larger and
more finished work. In Paris, during my
travels, in the country, these notebooks have
been carelessly scribbled in without a thought
for the future work which was accumulating
there; surnames are there too, which I have
been unable to change, finding in their very
sound a physiognomy, a living image of those
who bore them. On the publication of some

of my books there has often been an outcry
and a talk of a "key" to my novels; some
such thing has indeed been published, with
a long list of celebrated personages, without
reflecting that in my other works many real
characters have also figured, unknown, it is
true, and lost amongst the crowd where no
one has sought for them.

Is it not the true way to
write a novel, that is to say,
the history of those folk
who have no history? All
the individuals in *Fromont*
have lived or are still living.
By my delineation of old
Gardinois, I have grieved
some one for whom I
have a sincere affection,
but I could not omit this specimen of a
selfish and terrible old man, of the pitiless *parvenu*, who many a time from the
terrace in his park threw his covetous glance
over the large buildings of the farm and
manor, the woods and the cascades; and
said to his children assembled around him :
" What consoles me in dying, is that after

me not one of you will be rich enough to
keep all this together." Planus, the cashier,
was in real life called Scherer. I saw him
in a banking-house in the rue de Londres,
shaking his head in front of the well-filled

strong box, and muttering in a soft, tragi-
comic manner and strong uncouth Teutonic
accent: "*Fui, fui, te l'archent, peaucoup
l'archent; mais chai bas gonvianze* (" Yes, yes,
money, lots of money, but I've no faith in

it). Sidonie also exists, and the poor home of her parents, and Mother Chèbe's little case of diamonds, stored away in a corner of the Empire chest of drawers, for so long the only bit of luxury belonging to the Chèbe household. Only Sidonie was not so vile as I have drawn her. Full of intrigue and ambition, her head turned with her unexpected fortune, intoxicated with pleasure and dress, she was however incapable of behaving badly in her own home, in the way I have described,—with a view to scenic effect. Madame Gardinois still flashes and twirls her rings in the same manner far away in the provinces; but she will never read this book. She never reads; her fingers are too busy. Risler is a recollection of my childhood. That tall fair man, designing patterns in a manufactory, was employed by my father. I made him Swiss instead of Alsatian, in order not to pander to any patriotic sentimentality and call forth an easily-won applause. Finally, Delobelle lived near to me, and more than a dozen times has said to me : " I have no right to leave the stage." In him I have, in order to complete the type, summed up all I knew about actors—their

manias, the difficulty they find in resuming
every-day life when they leave the boards,
and in keeping their own individuality under
so many different garbs. I have here, amongst
old memoranda turned over while writing
this book, a "Blessing of the Sea," recited
by an actor, which is certainly one of the
most extraordinary things possible. I cannot
transcribe it here. It would be impossible
for me to describe the rolling of eyes and
voice, the maudlin emotion, the breathless-
ness, the quivering attitude of· tremendous
feeling that accompanied the delivery of this
curious declamation, heard in the greenroom
of the old Vaudeville theatre. Then again,
I find in a notebook a sketch of the wonderful attitude of another Delobelle, contemplat-
ing his house, burnt down by the Prussians,
rendering a very natural feeling of regret by
gestures so inappropriate as to be absolutely
comical; for it is the peculiarity of this class
whose study it is to interpret life that they
misunderstand everything and are never able
to divest themselves of the conventional stage
illusion, so devoid of light and shade. My
mind was therefore well impregnated by the
figure of Delobelle; but I had not yet con-

ceived him as completed by his family, when
about that time I assisted at the funeral of
a great actor's daughter; there I beheld in a
courtyard of the rue de Bondy the whole
theatrical world; and all that I describe
later on as taking place at the death of little
Désirée—the typical entrance of the guests,
the play of their different shake hands, varied
according to their habitual parts—the tear
wiped out of the corner
of the eye and gazed at
on the tip of the gloved
finger. I immediately
conceived the idea of
giving Delobelle a daugh-
ter and I was desirous of
describing that child as
having inherited some
of the oddity of the
father, transforming the artistic irritability
into the gentle sentimentality of the
woman and the invalid. By reason even
of this sickliness, and in contrast with it, I
bestowed upon her a trade devoted solely to
luxurious accessories. First, I made her a
doll-dresser, in order that this humble and
unfortunate girl might at least satisfy her

delicate and elegant taste, and in default of
herself, clothe her dreams in shreds of silk
and gold tinsel. The work was essentially
one of those practised in the buzzing, droning

Marais, in the old scutcheoned mansions and
black five-storied houses in which are sheltered those who prepare the pleasures of

Paris, letting fall in the dust of their garrets
or on the wrought-iron railings of their staircases bits of gilding and chips of veneering
woods.   Go into those narrow alleys, climb
up those melancholy stairs, through the half-
opened doors on each landing, you will see
women and children working round a wretched
fire by the light of a petroleum lamp.   A bit
of wire, a little glue, gilt paper, and a few
snips of velvet, are sufficient, notwithstanding
póverty and cold, for them to create with
their nimble fingers, almost without a tool,
by sheer dexterity and ingenuity, those little
trifles, "pretty and well-made," as the Boulevard street sellers say in offering their wares:
clowns, dancing dolls, butterflies with wings
that flutter, perfect marvels for twopence,
toys for the poor, made by the poor, bearing
the stamp of the delicate, childlike taste of
this wonderful Parisian population.

In relating my book out loud, as is my
custom while mentally evolving it, I mentioned one day to André Gill, the sketcher
of outlines, who was in all respects an artist.
the little Delobelle and the manner in which
I was describing her; and he warned me
that in one of Dickens's novels, till then

unknown to me, *Our **Mutual** Friend*, there
was exactly the **same** account **of an** infirm
girl, a doll dresser; described **with the deep**
tender sentiment **for the poor, the** imaginative
feeling for the street, which is **so palpable in**
the great English novelist.   **I remembered**
how often **I** had been compared **to Dickens,**
even long before a friend had, **on returning**
from a journey **in England, informed me of**
the sympathy existing **between *David Copper-***
field and *Le Petit Chose*.   **An author who**
conscientiously records **what he sees, can**
make no answer **to such a criticism, except**
that there are certain affinities **of the mind**
for which one is not **responsible, but that on**
the day of the great **creation of men** and
novelists, nature in a **fit of abstraction may**
have mixed her materials.   **I feel in my**
heart, **the** love **that Dickens felt for the**
unfortunate and the poor, and for **childhoods**
spent in the **wretchedness of large cities;**
like him, **I began life in a** heart-rending
manner, **obliged to gain my daily bread**
before **I was sixteen years of age; in that**
lies, **I** believe, **our greatest** resemblance.
Nevertheless, my conversation with Gill
threw me into a state of despair, and, giving

up doll dressing, I strove to find some other
trade for the little Delobelle. Such things
are not however easily invented; and then,
how should I be able to discover so practical
an imaginary profession as that of doll
dresser, showing all I meant to portray; the
exquisite grace in the wretched existence,
the smiling dream under the dingy roof, the
nimble fingers embodying the winged in-
spirations. Ah, how many of those sombre
houses did I not search through, how many
cold stairs, with their rope bannisters did I
not climb that year, while seeking for my
ideal home among the numberless paltry
little manufactories. At last I almost de-
spaired; but my obstinacy found its reward.
One day, rue du Temple, on a leathern
placard, in one of those frames on which
for the convenience of purchasers are written
and advertised all the trades carried on in
the house, I read in faded gilt letters. which
nevertheless dazzled me:

BIRDS AND FLIES FOR BONNETS.

THE habit I have already mentioned of relating my books aloud, is with me a process of my work. To explain to others my subject elucidates it to myself, I become more deeply imbued with it ; experiment upon my listeners what parts will tell, and the conversation brings me new ideas—godsends, which, thanks to my excellent memory, I am able to retain. Woe betide the luckless caller who rashly intrudes on my feverish creation! I continue mercilessly in his presence talking instead of writing, putting together anyhow, so that they may be somewhat intelligible to him, the different parts of my novel ; and in spite of the bored and absent looks with which he tries to fly from my superabundant improvisation, I build up my chapter and develop it in words. In Paris, in my study, in the country, in my strolls through the green meadows, and out boating, how many of my comrades have I not thus tired out, while they little guessed their part of silent collaboration. But my wife has had to bear the greater part of this repetition of outspoken work, of subjects thought over and over twenty times running. "How do you

think it would do to make Sidonie die?
Shall I let Risler live? What must Delobelle or Frantz or Claire say in such and
such a circumstance?" It went on from
morning till night, at each instant of the
day, at meals, on our way to the theatre,
on our return home from parties, during
those long cab journeyings through the
silence and slumber of
Paris.   Ah, the poor
wives of writers!   True,
mine is such an artist
herself, and has taken
such a part in all I have
written! Not a page she
has not looked over,
touched up, on which she
has not thrown a dash of her fine azure and
gold-dust. And withal so modest, so simple, so
little of a blue-stocking.   I expressed all this
one day, and rendered homage to all her
tender and indefatigable aid in a few dedi-
catory lines of the *Nabab;* but my wife would
not allow it to be printed, and I only left it on
a dozen copies given to intimate friends, now
very scarce, which I recommend to connoisseurs.

My method of work is known. All my
notes being jotted down, my chapters in
good order and well divided, my personages

thoroughly alive in my mind, I begin to
work quickly, rapidly. I dash down ideas
and events without allowing myself time for

proper or exact wording even, the subject
hurrying me on, swamping both details and
characters. The page covered, I hand it to
my collaborator; I look it over again afterwards; then at last I re-copy it; and with
what joy!—the joy of a schoolboy who has
finished his task, touching up some phrases,
completing, refining them; it is the best
period of work. *Fromont* was thus written
in one of the oldest palaces of the Marais,
where my study, with its large light windows,
looked out on the fresh green and the darkened trellis of a garden. But beyond that
zone of calm and of piping birds lay the
working life of the faubourgs, the straight
smoke of the factories, the rumble of the
vans, and I still hear on the pavement of
a neighbouring yard the rattle of a little
hand-cart, which at the moment of New
Year's gifts dragged about children's drums
from early morn till seven o'clock at night.
There is nothing more healthy, more exciting
than working in the very atmosphere of one's
subject, in the centre in which one's own
personages are living. The noise of the
workmen entering and leaving the mills, the

call-bells of the factories, ran through my
pages at fixed hours. No effort was required
to find the local colour, the ambient air;
I was invaded by it. The whole surroundings helped me, carried me away, worked
for me. At the two extremities of the large
room stood my long table and my wife's
little writing-bureau, and running to and fro,
carrying the sheets from one to the other,
my son, now a medical student, then a child
with thick fair locks falling over his little
pinafore, black with the ink of his first up-
and-down strokes. It is one of the happiest
recollections in my author existence.

Sometimes, however, I required some
more distant detail, an observation noted
down in some special place; then all the
family would start off in search of the impression. I dined with my wife and child
in the Palais Royal, the very dinner Risler
and Sigismond dined after they were ruined,
at the hour when the military music was playing, when the straw chairs placed in circles,
the tired attitudes of the people listening,
even the dripping of the fountains on the
dust of a hot summer's evening, threw out

a peculiar melancholy ; an emptiness, the provincialism of Paris in summer time. I felt thoroughly impregnated by it, and, wrapped up in my subject, stirred by the

hackneyed military music, I fancied it softly accompanying the mournful conversation of my two unhappy heroes. The death of Risler necessitated a still longer expedition ; I had in my mind a little house of the editor

Poulet-Malassis, far away near the fortifications, and I had settled Planus there in
front of green slopes, with yellow flowers
scattered and trodden down by the Sunday
excursionists.   It became necessary to revisit
that country, to follow Risler step by step,
from the threshold of the house to the dark

archway, where he was to hang himself, close
to those barracks, from whence one can
behold Paris, as it may be seen from the
suburbs : a smoky mass of tightly packed
cupolas, steeples and roofs, with a perspective
like that of an immense harbour, of which
the chimneys might be the masts.   Hence-

M

forth I had the outline of all my chapters.
I had but to write; and under these conditions, the drama pictured, illustrated, I
may say, by my recollections and my walks,
the work was already half done..

Fromont jeune et Risler aîné appeared in
feuilletons in the *Bien Public*, and during its
publication I felt, for the first time, that my
work awoke the serious interest of the public.
Claire and Désirée found friends; I was reproached with the death of Risler, and I
received letters interceding for the little lame
girl. Life offers nothing better than this
dawn of popularity, this first intimacy of
the reader and the author.

The book was published by Charpentier,
who had just moved into a bright apartment
full of sunshine, on the Quai du Louvre, a
charming and friendly home which has
become a regular literary *rendezvous.* It
was on leaving him, after one of the last
evenings of the season, towards the month
of May, that a perfectly clear vision of the
death scene of Désirée Delobelle occurred
to me, as I walked through the rows of
flowers ready for the morrow's market, while

before me lay the Seine, all starred with
reflections of the gas lamps.

The successful sale of the book astonished
me much. Accepted until then only by a
small artistic group, I had never dreamt of
any great popularity, and I well recall my
delighted surprise at the announcement of a
second edition which greeted me when, some
days after the publication of my book, I came
in fear and trembling to ask for news of it.

Soon reprints succeeded each other rapidly ;
then came a demand for translation from Italy,
Germany, Spain, Sweden, Denmark, from
England too, but last of all. It is the country
in which I have most slowly made my way, and
yet the one in which it would have seemed
that my choice of homely subjects would
have been most likely to attract and please.

One more detail.

At that time we used to have at Gustave
Flaubert's Sunday meetings, which by degrees
made of a little group of writers, united by
their respect and zeal for literature, a group
of true friends. We met in a suite of tiny
rooms in the rue Murillo, overlooking the
carefully trimmed clumps of shrubs, and the

sham **ruins** of **the** Parc Monceau. Within,
was the quiet of **a private** house opening on
to a park, and a freedom of artistic talk which
gave me pleasure of the highest and most re-
fined sort. The party was composed of four
of us, or perhaps five when Tourguéneff **was**
free from the gout, **and the** dinner which
brought us together **every** month was **boldly**
called " **the dinner** of unsuccessful authors ; "
at **it** we cursed the indifference of the age to
literature, and the timid reception given by **the**
public to **any new** departure. The fact is,
not one of us had the good luck to **catch** the
ear of **this** terrible public.

Flaubert was undergoing the melancholy
attendant on **past success, drunk** to the **very**
dregs, even **to the** reproaches of the **critics**
and the masses, always holding **up** the **first**
work as **a standard,** making of *Madame
Bovary* a glorious obstacle **to the** renown
of *Salammbô* or the *Education sentimentale.*
Goncourt seemed tired out, disheartened by
a strenuous effort which would profit **a whole**
fresh generation of novelists, and would leave
him, the instigator of it—or at least he thought
this would **be** the case—almost unknown.

Suddenly I found myself the only one of the party who could feel that fashion had turned towards him, with several thousand copies to prove the fact; and I was quite embarrassed by it, almost ashamed indeed, in the company of writers of such merit. Each Sunday when I arrived they would ask, " Well, and how about the editions ? What number have you got to now ? " Each time I had to acknowledge fresh reprints; honestly, I did not know where to hide myself and my success.   " Our books will never sell," Zola would say, without envy, but somewhat sadly.

It is twelve years since then.   Now his novels run to a hundred editions ; those of Goncourt are in every hand, and I smile when that plaintive and resigned accent recurs to me, " Our books will never sell."

TOURGUÉNEFF.

THE time is ten or twelve years ago, the scene Gustave Flaubert's home in the rue Murillo. The coquettish little rooms, hung with Oriental materials, opened upon the Park Monceau, that trim and aristocratic garden which held up a blind of greenery before the windows. There we met every Sunday, five or six of us, always the same, in a delightful intimacy. Strangers and bores were rigidly excluded.

One Sunday, when I came as usual to meet the old master and the expected friends, Flaubert seized upon me the moment I entered.

"You do not know Tourguéneff? There he is."

And without waiting for an answer he pushed me into the drawing-room. On a divan lounged a tall old man with a snow-white beard, who as I entered raised and uncoiled himself like a boa-constrictor with great astonished eyes from the pile of cushions.

It must be owned that we French live in extraordinary ignorance of all foreign literature. Our minds are as stay-at-home as our bodies, and with a horror of travel amidst the unknown, we read no better than we colonise, when we are taken out of our own country. As it happened, I knew Tourguéneff's writings well. I had read with the deepest interest the *Mémoires d'un Seigneur Russe*, and the study of this book had led me on to the knowledge of others. We had a link to bind us together, even before we became personally acquainted, in our common love of cornfields, of forest thickets, of nature in short—a twin comprehension of its penetrating charm.

Generally speaking, descriptive writers have only eyes, and are content to paint what they see ; Tourguéneff besides can smell and hear. All his senses have doors opening upon each other. He is overflowing with country scents, the noise of streams, clear skies, and allows himself to be lulled, without reference to any school, by the orchestra of his own sensations.

This music does not reach all ears. The denizens of cities, deafened from childhood by the roar of great towns, never perceive it. They fail to hear the voices which speak in the so-called silence of the woods, when nature fancies herself alone, and when man, holding his peace, has succeeded in being forgotten. Can you recall to yourself the splash of oars from a far-distant boat that you have heard in fancy on some lake of Fenimore Cooper's ? The boat is miles away, far beyond the range of vision ; but the woods seem to become the vaster for this far-off sound vibrating on the still waters, and we feel the thrill of solitude.

It was the Steppes of Russia that brought the heart and senses of Tourguéneff to blossoming point. One becomes good by listening to nature, and those who love her do not lose their interest in mankind. Hence that sympathetic gentleness, sad as a moujik's song, which seems to sob in the background of all Slave story-tellers' tales. It is the sigh of humanity spoken of in the creole song, the valve which saves mankind from suffocation : " *Si pas té gagné, soupi n'en mouné, mouné t'a touffé.*" And it is this sigh constantly re- peated which makes the *Mémoires d'un Seigneur Russe* a second *Uncle Tom's Cabin*, minus shrieks and declamations.

I knew all this when I met Tourguéneff. For a long time he had reigned in my Olympus on an ivory throne among the ranks of my deities. But far from suspect- ing his presence in Paris I had never even asked myself whether he were dead or alive. Imagine my astonishment when I found myself face to face with him in a Parisian drawing-room on the third floor looking on to the Parc Monceau.

I told him all this lightly and expressed my admiration for him. I told him, too, how I had read him in the woods of Sénart. There his spirit was so well in unison with the surroundings ; and the balmy remembrances of the landscape and of his books were so intermingled that more than one of his stories

was represented in my thoughts by the colour
of a little patch of pink heather already faded
by autumn.

Tourguéneff could not hide his astonishment.

"What! you have really read me?"

Then he gave me some particulars as to
the small sale of his books, and the obscurity
of his name in France. Hetzel had pub-

lished for him almost as a charity. His popularity had not gone beyond the frontier. It hurt him to live unknown in a country for which he had an affection, and he confessed his mortifications a little sadly, but without any bitterness. On the contrary our disasters of 1870 had only increased his attachment to France. He could no longer bear to quit it. Before the war he used to spend his summers at Baden, now he would no longer go there, but contented himself with Bougival and the banks of the Seine.

It happened on this particular Sunday that there was no one else at Flaubert's, and our *tête-à-tête* was prolonged. I questioned the writer upon his method of working and expressed my surprise that he did not make his own translations, for he spoke excellent French—a shade slowly, to give time for the subtle play of his mind.

He owned to me that the Académie and its Dictionary frightened him. He turned the leaves of that formidable dictionary in fear and trembling, as if it were a code wherein were formulated the laws of words and the penalties incurred for any hardihood

of expression. He emerged from these re-
searches with a conscience pricked by literary
scruples, which killed all energy and disheartened him for further attempts. I remember that in a novel he wrote about this
time he did not venture to risk the phrase,
"*ses yeux pâles*," through fear of the *Forty*
and their definition of the epithet.

It was not the first time I had met with
such anxieties. I had already found them
in my friend Mistral, who was also spell-
bound by the cupola of the Institute, that
ridiculous monument, a medallion of which
adorns the covers of the Didot edition

On this subject, I set forth to Tourguéneff
what I had so much at heart : that the
French tongue is not a dead language, to be
written with a dictionary of definite expressions, classified as in a Gradus. For
myself, I felt it to be instinct with life, a
grand river rolling along with a powerful and
scouring current, full to the very brink. The
river indeed picks up much dross by the
way, for everything is thrown into it, but let
it flow on, and it may be trusted to make its
own selection.

Then, as the day wore on, Tourguéneff observed that he must join "the ladies," at the Pasdeloup Concert, and I came away with him. I was delighted to find that he loved music. In France, literary men in general have a horror of it, painting having usurped its place. Théophile Gautier, Saint-Victor, Hugo, Banville, Goncourt, Zola, Leconte de Lisle, are all music haters. To the best of my belief, I am the first to confess aloud an ignorance of colour, and a passion for music ; no doubt this arises from my meridional temperament, and from my short sight, one sense has developed at the expense of the other. With Tourguéneff the taste for music had been part of his Parisian education. He had absorbed it from the surroundings in which he lived.

These surroundings had been formed by an intimacy of thirty years' standing, with Madame Viardot, Viardot, the great singer, Viardot-Garcia, sister to Malibran. A bachelor, and very lonely, Tourguéneff had lived for years in the family mansion, 50 rue de Douai.

"The ladies" of whom he had spoken

to me at Flaubert's, were Madame Viardot
and her daughters whom he loved as his
own children.   It was in this hospitable
dwelling that I visited him.

The house was furnished with refined
luxury, and a great attention alike to art and
to comfort.   In crossing the hall, I saw

through an open door, a gallery of paintings.
Fresh voices of young girls came to me
through the hangings, and alternating with
them was the sympathetic and powerful
contralto of *Orphée*, which filled the staircase
and ascended with me.

Up stairs, on the third floor, was a snug

little room, crowded as a boudoir, with soft and comfortable furniture. Tourguéneff had borrowed from his friends their artistic tastes; music from the wife, painting from the husband.

He was lying on a sofa.

I sat down by him, and we at once resumed the conversation begun a few days previously.

He had been struck with my remarks, and promised to bring to Flaubert's on the following Sunday, a story which should be translated under his own superintendence. Then he talked to me of a book he wished to write, *Les Terres Vierges,* a sombre picture of the new classes seething in the depths of Russia, the history of those poor *simplifiés,* pushed by a heartrending misunderstanding into the arms of the people. The people do not understand them, but repulse and jeer at them. And while he spoke I reflected that Russia is indeed a virgin land, an inchoate country, scarcely yet more than a marsh, whereon every footstep leaves its print, a country where all is new, all to be done, all to be explored. With us, on the

contrary, there is no longer even a deserted
avenue, a pathway that has not been trodden
underfoot by the crowd; and to speak only
of the novel writer's art, the ghost of Balzac
appears at the end of every alley.

After this interview our meetings became
frequent. Amongst all the hours spent together I have a vivid impression of a spring
afternoon, a Sunday in the rue Murillo,
which stands out in my recollections unique
and luminous. We had spoken of Goethe,
and Tourguéneff had said to us, " You know
nothing about him." The following Sunday,
he brought *Prometheus* and the *Satyr*, that
Voltairian tale, impious and rebellious, ex-
panded by Goethe into a dramatic poem.
From the Parc Monceau came to us the
cries and shouts of children, the clear sunshine, the freshness of the well-watered
lawns, and we four—Goncourt, Zola, Flaubert, and myself—moved by this magnificent
improvisation, listened to genius interpreted
by genius. This man, who trembled when
pen in hand, had, as he stood there, all the
splendid audacities of the poet; it was not
the misleading translation which curdles

and petrifies, but Goethe himself living and speaking to us.

Often too, Tourguéneff would come to seek me in the heart of the Marais, in the old hotel Henri II., where I then dwelt. He was amused with the strange sight presented by the great courtyard, the royal dwelling with its gable ends and *mashra-beyahs* filled with the petty industries of Parisian trade—manufacturers of tops, of seltzer-water and sugar-plums. One day, when he arrived—a colossal figure—arm-in-arm with Flaubert, my little boy said to me in a whisper, " Why, they are giants !" Yes, giants they were, excellent giants, with great brains and great hearts proportionate to their appearance. There was a link, an affinity of simple goodness between these two genial natures. It was Georges Sand who had united them. Flaubert, boaster and fault-finder, a Don Quixote with the voice of a trumpeter of the Guards, and his powerful irony of observation, his manners of a Norman of the Conqueror's time, was certainly the masculine half of this marriage of minds ; but who would have guessed that

in this other Colossus, with bushy eyebrows
and immense flat cheekbones, was the feminine element ; the woman of acute delicacy
described by Tourguéneff in his books ; that
nervous, languid, passionate Russian, sleepy
as an Oriental, tragic as a nation in revolt?
So true is it that in the vast confusion of the
manufacture of humanity souls occasionally
mistake their proper envelopes, and men's
souls may find their way to women's bodies,
while the souls of women may chance into
the carcases of cyclops.

It was at this date that the idea of a
monthly meeting, at which friends should
assemble at a good dinner, occurred to us.
It was to be called " the Flaubert dinner,"
or " dinner of unsuccessful authors." Flaubert was to be admitted, on the strength of
a slight check with his *Candidat ;* Zola on
account of *Bouton de Rose ;* Goncourt for
Henriette Maréchal ; myself for my *Arlésienne.* Girardin wished to insinuate himself
into our band, but he was not a literary
man, and we refused him admittance. As
for Tourguéneff, he gave us his word of
honour he had been damned in Russia, and

as it was so far off no one went thither to
ascertain the fact. Nothing could be more
delightful than these friendly dinners, where
we talked in perfect freedom, elbows on
table, our minds thoroughly roused to action.
As experienced people should be, we were
all *gourmets,* and so there were as many
pet dishes as there were temperaments ; as
many different recipes as there were provinces. Flaubert must have Normandy but-
ter and stewed Rouen ducks; Edmond de
Goncourt, exotic and refined, demanded preserved ginger; Zola, sea-urchins and cockles;
while Tourguéneff enjoyed his caviare.

Ah ! we were not easy to provide for,
and the restaurants of Paris no doubt remember us. We often changed our meeting-
place. Sometimes it was at Adolphe and
Pelé, behind the Opera ; sometimes in the
square of the Opera Comique ; then at
Voisin's, whose cellar could meet any emer-
gency and reconcile all tastes. We were
wont to sit down to table at seven o'clock,
and at two o'clock we had not finished.
Flaubert and Zola dined in their shirt-
sleeves ; Tourguéneff lounged on the divan ;

the waiters were turned out—a needless precaution, since Flaubert's "roar" could be heard from roof to cellar of the house —and we talked literature. There was always on the table a book by one or other of us at any rate, just out. It might be the *Tentation de Saint-Antoine* and the *Trois*

Contes of Flaubert; *La Fille Elisa* of Goncourt; *L'Abbé Mouret* of Zola; Tourguéneff brought *Reliques Vivantes* and *Terres Vièrges;* and I, *Fromont* or *Jack.* We opened our minds to one another without flattery and without any conspiracy of mutual admiration.

I have here before me a letter **of** Torgué-
neff's, the handwriting large, foreign, ancient
in appearance, **a** writing **of** old manuscript;
and this letter I transcribe **in its entirety, for**
it well describes **the tone of sincerity** prevailing amongst **us:**

"Monday, 24 *May,* '77.

"MY DEAR FRIEND,

"If I have not yet spoken **to you about**
your book, it is because I wished **to do so**
at length, and would not content **myself with**
a few commonplace phrases. I postpone **it**
all till our meeting, which **will soon** take
place now, I hope, since **Flaubert will** soon
return and our dinners **will recommence.**

"I will confine myself to saying one thing:
the *Nabab* is the most remarkable and also
the most unequal book you have written.
If *Fromont* and *Risler* were represented by
a straight line ———, the *Nabab* would have
to be figured thus : ᐱᐯᐱᐯᐱᐯᐱ, and the
heights of the zigzags could only be reached
by a talent of the first order.

"I beg your pardon for expressing myself
so geometrically.

" I have had a long and very violent attack of gout. I only went out yesterday for the first time ; and I have the legs and knees of an old man of ninety. I much fear I am become what the English call 'a confirmed invalid.'

"A thousand kind regards to Madame Daudet, and with a warm shake hands,

"I am,

"Yours ever,

"IVAN TOURGUÉNEFF."

When we had done with the books and the chief interests of the moment, the conversation became more general, and we returned to the ever-present themes and ideas of love and death.

The Russian stretched out on his sofa said not a word.

"And you, Tourguéneff?"

"Oh, I never think about death. In our country no one has any very distinct idea on the subject; it is a vague, distant notion, enveloped in the Slavonic mist."

That word revealed the whole temperament of his race and of his own genius. The

Slavonic mist floats over all his handiwork, softening it, throwing a hazy vapour over all; even his conversations seeming pervaded by it. What he related was hesitatingly and laboriously begun ; then all at once some clear and incisive word dispelled the clouds as by a flash of light. He described his Russia to us, not the historical and stereotyped Russia of the Bérésina, but a summerlike Russia, speaking of ripe cornfields and tender blossoms springing up under the April showers; *Little Russia*, full of the fresh budding forth of nature, of green grass sprouting up, and the hum of the busy bees. And so, as we are wont to devise some kind of local habitation, to imagine some alreadyknown landscape as the setting in which to frame the exotic stories we may hear, Russian life appeared to me through his narrative as a vast manorial existence, placed in an Algerian country with a surrounding of Arab encampments.

Tourguéneff talked to us of the Russian peasant: of his inveterate drunkenness, his benumbed conscience, his ignorance of liberty ; or else he would describe some brighter

scene, some charming idyl, some tender recollections, such as that of a miller's daughter
whom he had met while on a shooting expedition, and with whom he had for a while
fancied himself in love.

"What shall I give you?" he had often
asked her; and the pretty maid had answered
blushingly,

"Bring me some scented soap from the
city that I may perfume my hands, and then
you will kiss them as you do those of the fine
ladies."

After love and death we talked of illnesses,
of the slavery in which we drag about with
us our wretched bodies, like the convict's
cannon-ball at the end of his chain. The
sad confessions in fact of men past their
fortieth year! As for me, not yet a victim
to rheumatism, I laughed at my friends, at
poor Tourguéneff, who was a martyr to gout
and who came limping to our dinners. Since
then I have changed my tone.

Alas! death of which we were always
speaking soon came. First Flaubert was
taken. He was the soul, the link which
bound us together. Once he was gone our

life changed, and we only met from time to time, none of us having the courage to resume the meetings so sadly interrupted by mourning.

Some months later, Tourguéneff endeavoured to bring us together again; Flaubert's empty place was to be kept at our table, but his loud voice and hearty laugh were too sadly missing. They were no longer the dinners of former days. Since then I have met the great Russian novelist at an evening party at Madame Adams's; he had brought with him the Grand Duke Constantine, who on his way through Paris was anxious to meet a few of the celebrities of the day— a kind of living and eating Tussaud's exhibition. Tourguéneff was ill and depressed. His pitiless enemy the gout constantly confined him to his bed, and he begged his friends to come and visit him.

I saw him for the last time two months ago. The house was still full of flowers, of fresh voices down stairs, while up stairs my poor friend lay stretched out upon his sofa sadly changed and weakened. He was suffering acutely from an attack of *angina pectoris,* and from a wound caused by the excision of a tumour. The operation having been perfomed without the aid of chloroform, he gave me a painfully lucid account of it. First came a circular sensation, like that of peeling a fruit, then the sharp pain of cutting into the quick. He added :

" I analysed my sufferings, in order to describe them to you at one of our dinners, thinking you might find it interesting."

As he could still drag himself about a little he came down stairs to accompany me as far as the door. We entered his picture-gallery, and he showed me some paintings of the Russian school—a Cossack camp, waving cornfields, and glowing Russian landscapes, such as he described them.

Old Viardot was there ; he also seemed ill. In the next room Garcia was singing, and Tourguéneff, surrounded by the artistic associations he loved so well, smiled as he bid me good-bye.

A month later I heard that Viardot was dead and that Tourguéneff was dying. I could not believe this. It seemed to me that as long as a beautiful and powerful mind had not yet said its last word life must surely be prolonged for it. Fine weather and the balmy air of Bougival would give Tourguéneff back to us, but the friendly gatherings he so loved to attend were at an end for him.

Ah, those Flaubert dinners! We began them again the other day; there were only three of us![1]

While I am correcting the proofs of this article, which appeared a few years since, a book of *Souvenirs* is brought to me, in which Tourguéneff from the other side of the grave criticizes me without mercy. As an author, I am beneath all criticism; as a man, I am the lowest of my kind. My friends were well aware of it, and told fine stories about me. What friends did Tourguéneff allude to, and could they remain my friends if they held such an opinion of me? And himself, that excellent Slave, who obliged him to assume so cordial a manner with me? I can see him in my house, at my

[1] Written for the New York *Century Magazine* in 1880.

table, gentle, affectionate, kissing my children. I have in my possession many exquisite warm-hearted letters from him. And this was what lay concealed behind that kindly smile. Good heavens! how strange life is, and how true that charming word of the Greek language, EIRÔNEIA.

RICHARD CLAY AND SONS, LIMITED, LONDON AND BUNGAY.